DIESEL AND ELECTRIC MOTIVE POWER ON THE SOUTHERN

1980s TO PRESENT

DIESEL AND ELECTRIC MOTIVE POWER ON THE SOUTHERN
——— 1980s TO PRESENT ———

David Goodyear

AN IMPRINT OF PEN & SWORD BOOKS LTD.
YORKSHIRE – PHILADELPHIA

First published in Great Britain in 2025 by
Pen and Sword Transport
An imprint of
Pen & Sword Books Ltd.
Yorkshire - Philadelphia

Copyright © David Goodyear, 2025

ISBN 978 1 03610 907 3

The right of David Goodyear to be identified as author of this work has been asserted by him in accordance with the Copyright, Designs and Patents Act 1988.

A CIP catalogue record for this book is available from the British Library.

All rights reserved. No part of this book may be reproduced, transmitted, downloaded, decompiled or reverse engineered in any form or by any means, electronic or mechanical including photocopying, recording or by any information storage and retrieval system, without permission from the Publisher in writing. No part of this book may be used or reproduced in any manner for the purpose of training artificial intelligence technologies or systems.

Typeset in Palatino 10.5/13.5 by SJmagic DESIGN SERVICES, India

The Publisher's authorised representative in the EU for product safety is Authorised Rep Compliance Ltd., Ground Floor, 71 Lower Baggot Street, Dublin D02 P593, Ireland.
www.arccompliance.com

For a complete list of Pen & Sword titles please contact

PEN & SWORD BOOKS LIMITED
George House, Beevor Street, Off Pontefract Road, Hoyle Mill,
Barnsley, South Yorkshire, England, S71 1HN.
E-mail: enquiries@pen-and-sword.co.uk
Website: www.pen-and-sword.co.uk

or

PEN AND SWORD BOOKS
1950 Lawrence Rd, Havertown, PA 19083, USA
E-mail: uspen-and-sword@casematepublishers.com
Website: www.penandswordbooks.com

Contents

	Foreword	6
Part 1	Diesel and Electric Locomotives	10
Part 2	Diesel Multiple Units and Railbus	86
Part 3	Diesel Electric Multiple Units	109
Part 4	Electric Multiple Units	122
Part 5	Departmental and Civil Engineers' Trains	143
Part 6	Second Generation Electric Multiple Units	148
Part 7	Eurostar	190
	Finale	192
	Bibliography	197

Foreword

Having been based in north Liverpool for my sixth-form years and later as a student at Lancaster University, I only became fully aware of the characteristic features of the Southern network and its associated multitudinous fleets of trains when in my first teaching post in Bracknell. A tantalising glimpse was first offered by a day's 'Mystery Excursion' organised by British Rail's North West division in the Whit or May bank holiday of 1978. This ran from Lancaster to its destination which eventually was revealed as Brighton, with my first taste of the classic Class 33s provided by an example of the Class attached at Willesden Junction, thence singing its way through the Southern suburbs and past un-trodden branch lines awaiting exploring off the main line. While in Bracknell, there was always the lure of travelling on all the available curves, branch lines, main line and subsidiary routes originating at London Victoria and Waterloo via Clapham Junction along with the South Eastern section with all of the lines from London Bridge, Cannon Street and Charing Cross, which kept me busy with my camera. I had many further opportunities to revisit this jigsaw of inter-threading lines, as I kept contact with various friends who lived in the area and on the south coast. Network SouthEast days provided further opportunities to mop up lines not yet travelled on, when I could journey up from Honiton behind a Class 50, 47 or 33 to London and beyond, all of which helped cover those awkward stretches of line that so far had evaded me. Whilst my friends would, on such event days, boast of reaching the extremes of Southend or Southminster, I would be scurrying around those threads of Network SouthEast within the reach of London's termini serving the South and South East.

While I was familiar with the concept of third rail electric suburban commuter traffic in Merseyside and the Wirral, the relative novelty and busy traffic evident within the vast network of the Southern area was increasingly interesting to me, especially as this era saw the traditional first generations of EMUs becoming withdrawn and replaced with, in my eyes, less interesting and appealing newer generation units which seemed to lack character

FOREWORD • 7

and aesthetic design, and hence my interest became focused elsewhere. Locomotive-hauled trains in the region were becoming increasingly rare and remained more than plentiful just across the Channel.

Realistically, the traction evident on the Southern reflected the needs of the passenger traffic which was different from the other regions. Only a few long distance main lines required locomotives and hauled coaches; rather a plethora of electric units which served the commuter rush to and from London's southern home counties, many of which sat in sidings (and some still do) during the off-peak hours, not earning their way. Topographically, there are few heavy

Bincombe Tunnels, Saturday, 6 August 2022: Class 33/0 West Coast Railways 33025 leads 33029 with Pathfinder Rail Tours' 'Dorset Coast Express' from Burton upon Trent to Weymouth as it departs from the tunnels and descends to the coastal town.

Corfe Common, Swanage Railway, Saturday, 12 May 2012: Class 33/1 33111, preserved at the Swanage Railway, heads the 16.45 Norden to Swanage in this perfect re-creation of a scene from the era of BR Blue diesel locomotive hauled trains within the attractive backdrop of the Purbeck hills.

gradients to match those of the northern rails, excepting the short Folkestone Harbour branch and the exacting incline from Exeter St Davids to Exeter Central, although plenty of tunnels reflect the need to burrow through the North and South Downs, and we should not overlook the demanding gradients of Southern routes through the Downs as well as Dorset and Devon.

Always of interest was the use of Class 33 and 47/7 locomotives down to the south west, and Classes 33 and 73 on the lines to Bournemouth and Weymouth, the latter while the Class 432/438 4-REPs were taken out of service when their electric motors were being refurbished for use in Wessex Electrics class 442s ready for use in enhanced services provided to the newly electrified Bournemouth to Weymouth line. Some parcels trains still ran and freight on main lines to the ports provided extra interest, but the multitude of electric units limited variety. The interesting aspect about the Southern Region motive power was that it was territorial, thanks to the requirement for electric trains to remain within the live third rail network while carrying the substantial commuter traffic generated by London, whereas with other regions diesel multiple units (DMU) could be transferred anywhere in the UK and

the various diesels often strayed through and into other Regions, be it with freight or passenger traffic. Such a network of complex intertwining routes accommodating Southern Electric trains was also noticeably located to the south of the Thames, with a few exceptions, especially in the London area, whereas the area north of the Thames was and remains served by the extensive underground and overground London Transport network with its routes into the heart of the City. Meanwhile, the Class 73s were most efficient when drawing power from the third rail and the Class 33s handled traffic requiring movement beyond the limits of the third rail.

Consequently, photographic interest was found where semaphore signals, latticework footbridges, original station buildings and architecture added inspiration to record the trains fanning out across the region. Modern architecture has also added interest, with the area around Vauxhall most recently providing a cityscape with buildings of eye-catching design in which to frame the passing 'ordinary' units passing by.

I have provided here a variety of the types of locomotive and electric and diesel units caught on camera during the early 1980s where many of the earlier photographs feature what are now considered to be 'heritage' trains, some of which have not survived into preservation. Fortunately, several preserved lines in the southern area perfectly capture the character of the traditional southern branch line in the days of late steam and heritage diesels. Alongside such we can admire the meticulously restored station at Okehampton and ride from there along the reinstated line with regular timetabled trains to and from Crediton; yes, the Southern's tentacles reached that far! Bere Alston features as the most westerly point, as it was indeed passed by the daily diesel hauled service to Brighton, albeit until Saturday 4 March 1967, earlier than the scope of this book. Where a preservation location is given, it refers to the location at the time of the photograph – many locomotives transfer ownership or base of residence.

It is an interesting aspect of the changing nature of the railways during this century that several of the second generation of EMUs operated on the Southern have been withdrawn during the time of writing and replaced by technically more advanced train fleets. Time will tell how successfully they replace their predecessors, including the comfort and reliability that they are claimed to offer.

Part 1

Diesel and Electric Locomotives

Class 03

Remarkably, most diesel and electric traction on the Isle of Wight had previously operated either on the British Railways or London Transport networks, and this Class 03 was no exception, having been based at Darlington and Gateshead prior to its move south. In fact, the entire Class 03 fleet was operated within the Eastern Region of BR, and I recall a regular member of these lightweight locomotives buzzing around Hull station and environs whilst based at Hull Botanic Gardens depot. 03079 was newly delivered to Doncaster in January 1960 and saw allocation to several North Eastern depots including Darlington. It was transferred to Eastleigh in 1983 before moving across the Solent to the Isle of Wight where it resided at Ryde when this photograph was taken, being used for engineers' duties and consequently replacing Class 05 05001. The Isle of Wight line was a well-earned location to spend its final years of service, with a relatively quiet existence, seeing limited use. It can now be found on the Derwent Valley Railway in Yorkshire.

Sandown, Wednesday, 27 May 1992: Class 03 03079 in BR blue livery is seen stabled at the west side of the Up platform.

DIESEL AND ELECTRIC LOCOMOTIVES • 11

Class 08 and 09

Class 08 and 09 shunters have been well represented on the Southern, as also in all the BR Regions. Class 09s mainly saw use in Southern Region yards, where their versatility proved especially useful in shunting freight such as at Dover and Feltham, the latter's marshalling yards of which formed one of the largest in Britain, handling up to 7,000 wagons a day and hosting up to 80 steam locomotives in the steam era. Diesel shunters first made their appearance there in 1954. Diesel depots on the Southern Region at Eastleigh hosted the Class 08s and at Selhurst, Hither Green and Ashford the Class 09s. The latter could obtain a higher maximum speed of 27mph, but with a lower tractive effort compared to that of the Class 08s with their maximum speed of 20mph. Such proved useful for moving the locomotives between yards without hindering busy suburban passenger trains sharing the same lines. Eleven of this Class have been preserved – just under half of the total number built.

6695 was withdrawn from service at Cardiff Cathays shed in July 1964 and could certainly have rubbed shoulders with Class 08 shunters in service with BR, although not on Southern lines. This preserved railway scene therefore can facilitate recollections of the time when steam had yet to be fully replaced by the diesels, while

Corfe Common, Swanage Railway, Saturday, 12 May 2012: Class 08 08436 and 08476/D3591, both preserved at the Swanage Railway, pass with a late afternoon special from Norden to Swanage.

Corfe Castle, Swanage Railway, Sunday, 10 September 2006: Class 08 08436 is stabled, with the guard beckoning forward Great Western Railway (GWR) Class 5600 0-6-2T 6695 ready to collect a carriage, probably to strengthen one of the day's locomotive hauled services.

at the same time each locomotive pays tribute to a much older preserved symbol of cultural heritage, that of Corfe Castle which was built in 1280 in the reign of King Edward I.

Class 17

The adventurous timetable for the 2023 Swanage Railway diesel gala provided an hourly service from Swanage to the River Frome bridge, just south of Worgret Junction, and which was part of the line that was owned by Network Rail until September 2014 when the Swanage Railway took ownership of it. Train locomotives operated in top and tail mode for the purpose of the turn-around at that location, thereby extending the length of line beyond the customary limit at Norden for these events. This means that locomotives which are entirely disassociated with the relevant branch or region make rare or even unique appearances. This blue livery with a half-yellow box helps to remind us of the 1960s and early 1970s early modernisation era. Most survived for less than ten years in service, although D8568 escaped the cutter's torch by finding

DIESEL AND ELECTRIC LOCOMOTIVES • 13

Left and below: In the first picture, at the boundary of the Swanage Railway with Network Rail at River Frome, Saturday, 13 May 2023: Clayton Class 17 D8568 is seen departing with the 12.32 to Swanage, leaving a characteristic trail of diesel exhaust. In the second picture, at Corfe Common, Clayton Class 17 D8568 passes with the same train.

extended use when based at Hemelite Cement Company and later at Clitheroe with Ribble Cement. It spent its life at the latter in a distinctive Ribble Cement livery, and when first preserved – at the North Yorkshire Moors Railway – received a repaint into its original BR Green with half yellow box.

Class 20

Apart from some members of this Class owned by the private sector seeing use in the construction and electrification of High Speed One (HS1) through Kent, Class 20s generally stayed within their Eastern and Scottish region territory, some venturing over the Pennines to see use with coal trains serving Fiddler's Ferry Power station, West Lancashire. They were usually seen in pairs and have an interesting history. The first of the production batch of these English Electric Type 1 diesels, D8020-D8027, was delivered to the Eastern Region at Hornsey. The second batch was delivered to the London Midland Region (LMR) at Devons Road and Willesden. D8050-D8069 were delivered to the Eastern Region's Tinsley depot, where they became long established on freight duties throughout South Yorkshire. The Great Central Railway's Class 20, on loan to the Spa Valley Railway seen here, is one of the batch consisting of D8070-D8127 which were delivered to Glasgow Eastfield and Polmadie depots.

Forge Farm Crossing, Spa Valley Railway, Sunday, 25 October 2015: Class 20 D8098 approaches with the 14.20 Tunbridge Wells West to Eridge.

DIESEL AND ELECTRIC LOCOMOTIVES • **15**

Eridge, Spa Valley Railway, Sunday, 25 October 2015: Class 20 D8098 has arrived at the station with the above train on the line dedicated for Spa Valley Railway use, while the station canopy on the left covers the Network Rail station platform.

The locomotive's distinctive BR Green livery recalls the fact that this Class member was introduced to service in 1961, before any appearance of yellow panels on locomotives during the 1960s. At one time, situated on the left was a Crossing Keeper's cottage, with a hut for the keeper on the right. Home signals for Birchden Junction would have been visible in the distance.

Groombridge, Spa Valley Railway, Sunday, 25 October 2015: Class 20 D8098 heads past the station and signal box with the 12.15 service from Eridge to Tunbridge Wells West.

The Class 20 when running nose end forward is probably less appealing to the drivers than cab first, for practical reasons involving restricted sight of the route ahead. However, that is how they ran in service, especially when as a single loco. Their use in pairs on coal trains in Scotland was understandable owing to the weight of the consist, and this would most frequently see them operated nose to nose, but they also ran in single formation hauling a variety of wagonload goods such as the Aviemore to Craigellachie over the Great North of Scotland route. It is interesting that the Class saw a revival after their lives with BR had finished when Direct Rail Services (DRS) acquired fifteen. They later became a regular sight hauling nuclear flask traffic along the West Coast Main Line as well as that along the Cumbrian Coast line to and from Sellafield and as far west as Bridgwater for Hinkley Point power station. They also fulfilled duties with Rail Head Treatment Trains specifically during the autumn in Norfolk and Essex.

Enthusiasts of the Class have only to travel to Porto to experience travel behind the Portuguese Railways Class 1400 locomotives

DIESEL AND ELECTRIC LOCOMOTIVES • 17

Left and below:
First picture: Corfe viaduct, Swanage Railway, Sunday, 11 May 2008: Class 20 20096, in Railfreight Metals and Automotive decals, at the time preserved at Barrow Hill, leads the 16.50 Norden to Harmans Cross.
Second picture: Corfe Common, Swanage Railway, Sunday, 11 May 2008: Class 20 20096 is seen hauling the delayed 12.50 Norden to Harmans Cross.

which are based on the Class 20s. They operate most trains from Porto to Pocinho and their exhilarating sound fills the Douro Valley as purely as any of the UK Class 20s, amidst stunning scenery.

On 15 October 1987, the Trainload Business Sectors were formed. Trainload Freight constituted four sub-sectors: coal, petroleum, metals and construction. Each sub-sector of the operation was given their own two-colour roundel design of two overlapping squares. To be accurate, from the Class 20 fleet, only 20088 wore this livery during the time of BR Railfreight. More often, the traditional livery of Railfreight grey, yellow and red was applied. The intention of the sub-sector customisation was to provide a uniform livery for the Railfreight fleet which allowed some detail difference for the various depots which had previously applied their own depot emblems and paintwork adornments to characterise locomotives thus allocated to them. As a result, cast depot plaques and emblems were permitted within the strictures permitted by the new united Railfreight sector. Each depot was assigned its own symbol to apply to their fleet. The centralised intention was to maintain a unity of

Corfe Common, Swanage Railway, Saturday, 9 May 2009: Class 20 20107, owned by Harry Needle Railroad Company and reinstated to traffic on hire to GB Railfreight 31 May 2009, hauls the 13.30 Norden to Harmans Cross. At the rear is Class 33 33111. Within the train consist can be seen Class 117 Pressed Steel DMU DMBS (Driving Motor Brake Second Saloon) 51346 and DMS 51388, preserved at the Swanage Railway. The Isle of Purbeck hills stand proud in the background.

approach, although this was not helped by the fact that Thornaby's allocation of locomotives in particular embraced several sectors including petroleum, chemical, steel and Speedlink. The question then was: which logo to apply?

Pictured opposite, this Class 20 looks smart wearing BR Blue livery and appropriate disc headcodes. These served the same purpose as oil lamps mounted at the front of steam locomotives and indicated the class of train, such as 'empty coaching stock' seen here (passengers were on board, of course, as it was for demonstration purposes only). The use of such discs was replaced by a four-character headcode and this became redundant when headcodes were abolished in the mid-1970s and wound to '0O00' and, in time, plated over. Signal box staff no longer needed to see the codes for train identification purposes and many small signal boxes were replaced by centralised power signalling and modern telecommunications systems. The exception to the rule was in the Southern Region where timetables were intense and railway junctions necessarily complex. Here it was considered that the use of headcodes would still be beneficial in indicating a train's route, and consequently a six lamp/disc system was used.

Class 25

The Class 25s were very much a locomotive inhabiting the BR London Midland, Scottish and Eastern regions, with several providing service to the Western Region, and they would have reached the Southern in the late 1970s and early 1980s, working freights from the freight yards of North London, such as cement 'Presflos' from Willesden Sudbury Sidings to Norwood Yard. Traipsing the West London line, these trains had to negotiate the busy passenger network at both the north and south end, especially around Clapham Junction and Wandsworth Road. D7657 did work some trials along the former London and South Western Railway's (LSWR) Exeter to Barnstaple route prior to their approval for use in the South West. The earlier design Class 24 locomotives, equipped with the same Sulzer diesel engine as the Class 25, did see occasional use on the Southern early in their careers when the Southern Region borrowed sixteen to use in multiple on the South Eastern Division. The main problem that arose from such use was the fact that paired Class 24s were overweight for the routes intended, and their steam generating equipment had to be removed to reduce such weight, consequentially their use on

Groombridge, Spa Valley Railway, Sunday, 25 October 2015: Class 25 D7612/25262 arrives with the 12.20 Tunbridge Wells West to Eridge.

passenger trains henceforth was restricted to the summer months. In pairs they could be observed powering such services as Down relief boat trains to Dover or summer timetabled Margate to Birkenhead cross-country trains.

Class 26 and 27

Most associated with the Scottish Region following British Rail's evaluation of the performance and design of the Class 24, 25, 26 and 27 locomotives, many of these latter two Classes of locomotives first commenced service nearer to London. The initial batch of the Class 26s could be found working commuter services at the south end of the East Coast Main Line into London King's Cross while based at Hornsey; later batches were delivered directly to Haymarket, Edinburgh. Of the Class 27s, the first batch was delivered to Eastfield in 1961, whilst a substantial number from later batches delivered in 1962 worked Cross-London freight when

DIESEL AND ELECTRIC LOCOMOTIVES • 21

based at Cricklewood, and also saw use on passenger services including Tilbury Boat trains (although a small number were initially based at Thornaby depot, Teesside). Thereafter, from the late 1960s, both Classes 26 and 27 kept territorially to their Scottish duties with Carlisle as a southern-most boundary. However, they did share one thing with the Southern Region's diesel fleet and that was their common heritage with the Class 33s in being built at the impressive works of Birmingham Railway and Carriage Company (BRCW). They shared almost exactly the same Sulzer 6LDA28 engines which provided power, and also the transmission provided by four Crompton-Parkinson traction motors (Class 26 only; GEC for Class 27) – and they certainly sounded like the Class 33s, although bodywork design differences, especially with reference to the cab with its half-depth centre window, and the significantly lower power output of the Class 26/27, meant that they were not exactly the same.

Corfe Common, Swanage Railway, Saturday, 9 May 2009: Class 26 26007 powers past with the 13.10 Norden to Swanage, with the Isle of Purbeck hills in the background.

22 • DIESEL AND ELECTRIC MOTIVE POWER ON THE SOUTHERN 1980s TO PRESENT

Right and below:
First picture: Corfe Common, Swanage Railway, Saturday, 12 May 2012: Class 27 D5401/27056, preserved at the Great Central Railway, passes with the 16.28 Swanage to Norden.
Second picture: from the other direction, Class 27 D5401/27 056, approaches with the 17.30 Norden to Swanage.

The Class 27s impressed with their performance when working the dedicated Edinburgh to Glasgow InterCity push-pull expresses in the 1970s, which consisted of six Mk 2f coaches and a Class 27 at each end. The locomotives supplied required air-operated brakes to facilitate the high-speed braking from their scheduled fast running. Each locomotive cab was equipped for single man operation which meant the leading locomotives acquired through-train engine control. The intense diagram required twenty-four locomotives and thirty-six coaches – a heady demand indeed. The Class 27 versatility was also demonstrated by their use on the West Highland line's challenging gradients and the rolling Dorset countryside seen here near Corfe Castle provides a reminder. The green and yellow livery with white striped line along the body provides an admirable tribute to that 1960s colour scheme.

Class 31

In the early 1980s, the Exeter to Barnstaple branch saw Class 31 locomotives hauling 5-carriage sets of BR Mk 1, usually Saturdays only. Certainly by 1986 the use of Class 31s on a passenger train this far west would have been a rare occurrence, especially on the London Waterloo to Exeter route and this train is likely to have been booked for a Class 33 or Class 50. Perhaps before this occasion a rostered Class 33 working a Bristol to Portsmouth Harbour service via Salisbury had failed or experienced a problem and hence Bristol Bath Road substituted a Class 31, which at the time was known to occur. Subsequently, after returning to Salisbury from Portsmouth

Whimple, Saturday, 22 November 1986: Class 31/4 31406 departs with the 06.09 Salisbury, 08.08 Whimple to Exeter formed of Mk 1 coaches.

Corfe Common, Swanage Railway, Saturday, 9 May 2009: Class 31 31108, preserved at the Midland Railway Centre, with the 12.30 Norden to Swanage seen passing Corfe Castle.

it was more than likely 'borrowed' while laying over at Salisbury to operate the service seen in this photograph. Such is conjecture, but no doubt the residents of the nearby house were not too concerned with the unusual nature of this passing train!

Class 31 31108 is one of the Brush Type 2 locomotives of the British Rail Modernisation Plan, which were built from 1957 until 1962 and were designed for mixed traffic. The initial batch of twenty locomotives were built with a Mirrlees JVS12T 1,250hp engine, and the remaining 244 were fitted with uprated English Electric 12SVT motors providing 1,470hp along with the Brush transmission which serves individual traction motors on the outer axles of each bogie. As D5526, 31108 entered service at Stratford depot, and saw allocation to Finsbury Park, March, Immingham and Tinsley, and it was finally withdrawn in 1991. It is seen here restored in early Railfreight livery of light grey with 'wrap around' yellow cabs recalling its final BR colour scheme.

DIESEL AND ELECTRIC LOCOMOTIVES • 25

Class 33

This famed signal box was built on a bridge comprising two 120ft long steel main girders and spanned the Up and Down Windsor through and local lines, the two Kensington lines and three sidings. It was opened by the LSWR in 1912 and closed in 1990. The framing around the buildings on the gantry was provided in order to roof over the building during the Second World War for air raid protection. Track Circuit Block applied on the main running lines, but two Southern Railway three-wire, three position block instruments controlled the Absolute Block sections to Longhedge Junction and Latchmere Junction. The signal box made the headlines when in May 1965 the steel gantry supporting it partially collapsed early on a Monday morning, causing a total blockage to all services. Corrosion to the steelwork at one end of the gantry was the chief cause. The lever frame was undamaged, although full repairs to the signal box saw the wartime steel roof removed.

The Class 33/1 locomotives were a derivative of the standard BRCW Class 33 design, being equipped for push/pull services. They were part of the batch numbered 33 101 to 119. These locomotives became well established in working the Bournemouth to Weymouth portion of trains which arrived at Bournemouth from London Waterloo propelled by third-rail electric powered Class 432

Clapham Junction
'A' Signal Box, Friday, 7 April 1989: Class 33/2 33204 approaches with an RMC Aggregates train, while Class 421/2 4-CIG 1213 passes with a train heading for the South Coast.

Clapham Junction, Saturday, 10 August 1991: Class 33/1 33102 awaits movement with empty coaching stock; on the left a Class 73, light engine, appears to have started its diesel motors in a non-electrified siding.

4-REPs attached to one or two 4TC sets. One of the Class 33/1s would then attach to the stock at the country end of the train, after the 4-REP had detached, and take the train forward to Weymouth which was the terminus of the Dorset main line. This involved a heavy 1-in-50 gradient up past Upwey to Bincombe tunnels.

The Network SouthEast liveried General Utility Van (GUV) behind the Class 33 stands out against the InterCity liveried set of coaches which are clean and free of graffiti which has become a problem when tagging sets of coaches has spoilt the appearance of trains where inadequate security has allowed graffiti artists access to yards and depot perimeters. Fortunately, this has not applied in such vast quantities in Britain as it did to German and Italian railways in the same era as this photograph.

Comparison between this Type 3 Class 33 in service with the white cab surround, small yellow warning panel and full length white band and the similar livery worn in preservation by Type 2 Class 27 D5401/27056 as seen on page 22 shows how much of a family resemblance there is between these BRCW steeds, and how well the preservation era recalls the colours of the earlier BR colour schemes. With 27056 built in 1962 and 33008 built in 1960,

DIESEL AND ELECTRIC LOCOMOTIVES • **27**

their design is clearly similar, while the headcode box carried by the Class 27 was not required by the Class 33 as in its place they carried two-digit headcode blinds in the centre cab window. The Class 33 locomotives were more powerful than the Class 26 and 27, with an engine rated at 1,550hp. 33008 was the first of the Class to be named, at a ceremony at Eastleigh, its home depot, 11 April 1980.

Through the 1970s, Class 33s D6500/01/03-49/80 and D6555-75/77-79 and 81-97 were permanently allocated to Eastleigh and Hither Green respectively, usually with a seasonal move of D6550-54 between the two to facilitate Eastleigh's need for more locomotives during the summer season. Five basic coaching sets were based at Newton Abbot, branded 'to work between Waterloo and Exeter only' as a consequence of their non-standard electric train heating. Noteworthy was the through Brighton to South Devon train which ran until 1971 and which was hauled by two Hither Green based Class 33s.

The Class 33s certainly spread their wings in the late 1980s and early '90s, with the Southern route to Exeter seeing more of their use infilling between the Class 47/7s that more often provided the motive power for this demanding route. With fast running required

Woking, Saturday, 28 May 1988: Class 33 33008 *Eastleigh* passes through light engine.

Woking, Saturday, 24 October 1992: Class 33/1 33114 *Ashford 150* in NSE livery with the late running 09.51 to London Waterloo, 06.45 from Exeter St Davids, with a load of eight coaches including an ex-First Class MkIIF immediately behind the loco.

from Salisbury to London Waterloo and hefty gradients such as the several sections at 1 in 80 which clamber from Seaton Junction up Honiton incline, the Class 33s struggled to keep up with schedules previously prescribed for Class 50s. It is likely that, given autumnal issues with mulched leaves on the railhead, the reason why this train ran late is probably a combination of the lighter weight of the Class 33 and the above circumstances, thus 33114 has lost time as it has journeyed along the route with its many stations at which to call.

At the time of this photograph, the Class 33/0s were all based at Eastleigh with some out-stabled at Salisbury, and at this date they provided a dedicated service working the Portsmouth-Bristol-Cardiff trains, and also around the same time they could be seen in charge of Cardiff to Crewe services. Their appearance on the London Waterloo to Exeter route at this time was often a consequence of the rostered Class 50s failure – and that was quite frequent. Mk II stock provided a decent quality of ride, and of course the windows could be slid across for the purpose of listening to the Cromptons (a popular name given to the Class recalling their Crompton-Parkinson Transmission) slogging up and down the Wiltshire and Dorset countryside. They did perform reliable service on the route between

DIESEL AND ELECTRIC LOCOMOTIVES • 29

1971 and 1980, especially working the London Waterloo to Salisbury trains that filled the gaps between those trains voyaging the much greater distance to Exeter. With the arrival of the Class 50s, displaced Class 33s were moved over to the Portsmouth-Bristol service. The move of the Class 50s to the route was not necessarily welcomed by Southern Region management, some of whom considered them sufficiently heavy to give the permanent way such a pounding that it required much greater remedial attention!

BR blue livery certainly looked attractive on the Class 33s and helped this red nameplate and crest to stand out (page 30); 33027 received this name on 16 September 1980. Along with 33056 this locomotive in immaculate paintwork headed Lord Mountbatten's funeral train from London Waterloo to Romsey on 5 September 1979. 33056 later received the name *The Burma Star* on 1 September 1980. This Class 33/0 was based at Eastleigh, although earlier on in their career some were also to be seen based at Hither Green and Stewarts Lane.

Seen here carrying 'Triple Grey' silver and grey livery with Mainline branding, 33063 was delivered in January 1962 to Hither Green as one of this Class specifically delivered to the Southern

Crewkerne Station, Thursday, 24 May 1984: Class 33/0 33051 with the 18.32 from Crewkerne to London Waterloo.

30 • DIESEL AND ELECTRIC MOTIVE POWER ON THE SOUTHERN 1980s TO PRESENT

Region, and these locomotives certainly reached the limits of Southern branch lines in Sussex with evening rush hour trains as far as East Grinstead. 33063 was preserved after withdrawal in 1997 and saw service on the East Kent Railway until 2002 when it was moved along with 33065 to the Spa Valley Railway where

Gillingham, Sunday, 2 August 1987: Class 33/0 33027 *Earl Mountbatten of Burma* with the 14.10 London Waterloo to Exeter St Davids.

Eridge, Spa Valley Railway, Sunday, 25 October 2015: Class 33/0 33063 prepares to depart with the 15.15 to Tunbridge Wells West.

DIESEL AND ELECTRIC LOCOMOTIVES • 31

it has received bodywork restoration and a repaint into 'Triple Grey' with Construction Sector decals. 33063 looks at home in this purely Southern station with the preserved line on the left. Even the National Rail line on the right is still bestowed with a traditional platform canopy. At one time there were refreshment rooms with cellars beneath. The way that the station was signalled meant that terminating trains from Tunbridge Wells had to arrive at the Down bay but depart for Tunbridge Wells from the Up bay which required a shunt between the two across the 'main' Uckfield line.

Opened in May 1840, Micheldever station has an interesting history. Post-war, quarrying was used to house a major depot for aviation fuel. Thirty 650-tonne tanks were installed with a capacity of 7.5 million gallons, protected by 50ft of concrete and earth. After the First World War, it was here that chalk was quarried at the rate of 5,000 tonnes per week to reclaim land for expanding Southampton Docks. Such busy railway traffic moving the quarried chalk south was counter-balanced with up to 100 wagons per day carrying imported bananas.

The Type 3s began to dominate freight traffic in Kent early in their careers and from February 1961 they handled all freight on

Micheldever, Tuesday, 9 August 1988: Class 33/0 33060 leading, with second, 33012 pass through with a mid-afternoon southbound stone and ballast train.

the Hundred of Hoo branch, including the cement traffic from Cliffe and oil trains from the Grain. The Type 3s first appeared at Eastleigh Depot in July 1962 when twelve were transferred in to haul oil traffic from the Fawley refinery.

It is interesting to note that when introduced to passenger service on the South Eastern division, the Class 33s, equipped only with electric train heating, could be observed double-heading with Class 24s, the latter required for steam heating some of the more elderly coaching stock . In order to fulfil this purpose, some of the batch on loan to the Southern were returned to Derby for their steam heating to be restored. This avoided the problem of pairing Class 24s which when together exceeded weight restrictions in parts of the Southern – hence the appearance of Class 33s, with higher power output, paired with Class 24s.

This Class 33 has completed its clamber up the three miles of steep gradients, at 1 in 50 at their steepest, on Upwey bank and no doubt provided much amusement to any enthusiasts on board enjoying the sound of the Sulzer engine working hard. The Class 33 will detach from the 4TCs at Bournemouth while the 4-REP (Restaurant Electro-Pneumatic Brake) attaches to power the train

Bincombe Tunnel (south portal), Saturday, 25 October 1986: Class 33 33119 pushes 2 x 4TCs on the 12.32 Weymouth to London Waterloo.

forward to London Waterloo. This section of line is shared with GWR services as far as Dorchester, where they proceed towards Yeovil, Castle Cary and Westbury. On Summer Saturdays in steam days, two banking locomotives were kept at Weymouth for piloting trains up the steep grade as far as Dorchester South, with some trains continuing onto the Western Region route also provided with a banker as far as Bincombe signal box. It was not unknown for a rebuilt 'Merchant Navy' to provide such banking to another 'Merchant Navy' as train locomotive – what an impressive sight and sound that must have been!

May 1988 saw the completion of the installation of the third rail along the Dorset main line from Bournemouth to Weymouth, and in this scene the Class 33 is no longer required to power the 4TCs as far as Bournemouth, undertaking a duty which occupies Southern rails only as far as Dorchester. The newly introduced Wessex Electrics Class 442s will appear on all London services while the humble Class 423 4-VEP provides the stock for the stopping service to Bournemouth.

Certainly the Channel ferry Weymouth boat trains making their way along the quay past busy pubs and shops accompanied by

Weymouth, Saturday, 23 July 1988: Class 33/1 33112 *Templecombe* is seen attached to Class 438 4-TCs 8020 and 8025 forming the 17.00 Weymouth to Bristol Temple Meads. On the left is Class 423 4-VEP 3078 with the 17.15 Weymouth to Bournemouth. This is post-electrification.

Weymouth Quay Station and Custom House, Saturday, 26 September 1987: Class 33/1 33116 with Class 412/3 4-BEP 2305 forming the 18.55 service to London Waterloo.

rail officials carrying a folded red flag while walking ahead of the train provided much interest to holiday makers as well as local folk – and no doubt the British Transport Police who had to deal with recalcitrant badly parked cars blocking the way of the train. Locomotives were usually provided with a flashing light and bell unit to add warning devices for assisting the transit of the train. The bell did not ring continuously but could be controlled by the locomotive driver. The Weymouth Harbour Tramway, in its earlier years, featured some sidings and loops for freight trains that used it, with double track laid at Quay Station in use until 1961. Regular services to the quay ended shortly after the time of this photograph, although a number of special trains were permitted down the route in the 1990s. Unfortunately, the rails which remained alongside the quay were deemed a safety hazard for cyclists and pedestrians and the rails were eventually removed in October 2020. Some of the 4-CEPs (Corridor Electro-Pneumatic Brake) were provided with a buffet car in place of the second class open trailer and after refurbishment were re-classified as 4-BEPs (Buffet Electro-Pneumatic Brake), as seen here.

Double heading of Class 33s on the Southern was not always a frequent event. Regular double heading by Class 33s to increase loads on the Waterloo to Exeter route was impractical owing to the

DIESEL AND ELECTRIC LOCOMOTIVES • 35

Upwey Bank, Saturday, 6 August 2022: Class 33/0 West Coast Railways owned 33029 leads 33025 with the return Pathfinder Rail Tours' 'Dorset Coast Express' to Burton upon Trent.

platform length limitations at Waterloo. Two Class 33s standing on the buffer stops and two Class 33s at the head end for departure would need a train to be limited to eight coaches. However, the 13.00 Waterloo to Exeter was frequently double headed to Salisbury by Class 33s running in off classified repairs at Eastleigh Works. In the early 1980s, Class 33s were regularly in charge of the Brighton to Exeter services, with Hither Green allocated locomotives in charge. Double-heading by Class 33s running in from Eastleigh works tended to be most frequent on the 14.10 Waterloo to Salisbury. Fortunately, with accelerated services in the early 1980s, a full hourly service using Class 33/1 and TC sets was possible and consequently implemented between Waterloo and Salisbury.

In Dorset the Class 33s could be seen in pairs hauling the heavy tanker trains originating at Furzebrook oil terminal, at the north end of the Swanage branch, to Llandarcy. They were also responsible for hauling Summer Saturday Brighton to Exeter services, and as mentioned, operating Exeter to London Waterloo services in place of Class 50s in the late 1980s and early '90s as I have seen. In the South Eastern Division they could be seen hauling train loads of HAA merry-go-round coal hopper wagons from Ashford to Tyne Yard. Inevitably they also featured in moving Civil Engineers' trains around the Region.

The BR blue livery with full yellow cab as worn by 33111 was very much the standard for the Class after the era of BR green. It is a popular livery chosen for those examples that are preserved and it fits well with the authentic two character headcode panels and roller blinds with which they were bestowed for reasons explained previously. The locomotive has a fully overhauled power unit and traction motors. It was introduced to traffic in 1960 and allocated firstly to Hither Green and then to Eastleigh from December 1964. The Class 33s were provided with duplicate driving controls on each side of the cab, which assisted in shunting manoeuvres and such duties as those required by the Weymouth Quay operation of the boat trains

Seen in fine mid-Spring early evening sunlight crossing this Grade II listed viaduct (built 1885) striding over Studland Road, here's a chance to compare and contrast the two liveries of BR blue

River Frome, boundary of the Swanage Railway with Network Rail, Saturday, 13 May 2023: Class 33/1 33111 at the rear of the 12.32 to Swanage, which was departing behind the Class 17 seen in the picture on page 13.

DIESEL AND ELECTRIC LOCOMOTIVES • 37

and earlier BR green. D6515 was based at several depots during its service life, starting at Hither Green in 1960 before spending time at Eastleigh and Stewarts Lane. The locomotive gleams proudly as superbly restored, seen here carrying small yellow front panels and white cab window surrounds and silver roof, along with a white mid-body stripe recalling the livery variation worn by 33008 as seen at Woking, Saturday, 28 May 1988 featured on page 27.

At the top of page 38 we see 33012 looking equally smart fourteen years earlier than the previous photograph and looking very much the part in the Dorset scenery with the prominent chalk downs of the Purbeck Hills forming a backdrop. Class 33s did appear on the Swanage Branch in the BR era, working such trains as a mid-afternoon train formed of a 4TC set from London Waterloo and the early evening return service from Swanage to Bournemouth in the summer of 1969. In the unfortunate circumstances of the closure by BR of the Swanage branch, it was also a member of this Class, D6580, which performed the dubious honour of working the final train, a

Corfe Viaduct, Swanage Railway, Saturday, 7 May 2022: Front: Class 33/0 D6515/33012 *Lt Jenny Lewis RN* leads 33/1 33111 with the 18.15 Norden to Swanage.

Corfe Common, Swanage Railway, Sunday, 11 May 2008: Class 33/0 D6515/33012 is seen hauling the 14.30 Norden to Swanage.

Corfe Common, Swanage Railway, Saturday, 9 May 2009: At the rear (nearest camera) is Class 33 33103 *Swordfish*, preserved at the Swanage Railway; at the front is Class 33 33111, also preserved at the Swanage Railway, with the 12.25 Harmans Cross to Norden. Class 117 Pressed Steel DMU, DMBS 51346 and DMS 51388, is within the train consist behind 33111.

works train consisting of a steam crane and flat wagons, 23 June 1972. In 2022, D6515 received much needed repair to its bodywork, carried out at Arlington Fleet Services' Eastleigh Works, and a renewed livery of BR green with small yellow warning panels was applied.

This is probably an unrivalled example of Elysium for Class 33 enthusiasts – Southern Region heritage diesels at the front and rear of a train on Southern territory, both in immaculate BR blue, passing an icon of historic grandeur amidst Dorset's rolling hills, all complemented with gorse blossom in full regalia and in perfect sunshine. All that and a journey for the lucky passengers from the seaside up an impressive gradient with climbs of up to 1 in 76 helping to provide sound value from the relevant locomotive. Photographers and those filming the passing train will be equally delighted.

This is nearly a perfect recreation of a Class 33 hauling a 4TC set along the Swanage branch during the BR era, although in fact it is one of the suburban Wimbledon-based electric units that would have been more familiar on the rails to the south west of London, including the Waterloo to Reading route. The blue livery looks a fine match to that applied at the time of the transition from BR green to blue, and there is even a tribute to the first class section that is defined by the horizontal yellow line above the rear windows of the leading carriage. Interestingly, in the early 1970s

Corfe Common, Swanage Railway, Sunday, 11 May 2008: Class 33/0 D6515/33012, preserved on the Swanage Railway, hauls the 15.50 Swanage to Norden, formed of Class 423 4-Vep 3417 in BR blue, owned and restored by South West Trains for the latter days of slam-door workings.

one of the morning commuter trains from Salisbury to Basingstoke and evening commuter services from Waterloo to Salisbury was provided with a push/pull Class 33/1 and 8TC formation.

Delivered new in July 1960 and allocated to Hither Green shed, 33103 was reallocated to Eastleigh in 1966 and there it was converted to push-pull in October 1967. It actually wore 'Dutch' (Civil Engineers) livery in the early 1990s and saw withdrawal from service in 1993. Surprisingly, it was reinstated to service in February 1994 at Eastleigh, although it was stored out of use after a year, and ended its career at Stewarts Lane depot in February 1997. Now over sixty years old, it was just four months short of being of the same age as the final steam locomotive to be built for BR which was 9F 92220 *Evening Star*. Depending on trailing tonnage, some of the freights passing over the West London line in the early 1980s would have required banking assistance from Viaduct Junction (between Olympia and Willesden) including workings from north Kent such as bulk cement hauls and block tanker trains from Grain to Burn Naze. Pairs of Class 33 or 25 would have seen such use.

It is worth noting that, whilst the Class 33/0s were based at Eastleigh, in the privatised era that same depot became a home to classes of locomotive which had never been associated with this Southern facility. This includes some Class 37 and 58 locomotives, the latter displaced from coal train duties by the new Class 66s

From 1998, the Class 33s became synonymous with workings from and to Meldon Quarry working either singly or in pairs. As many as three or four such loadings per weekday could be

Corfe Common, Swanage Railway, Saturday, 9 May 2009: Class 33/1 33103 *Swordfish*, preserved at the Swanage Railway, with the 11.10 Norden to Swanage. The village of Kingston is seen in the background.

DIESEL AND ELECTRIC LOCOMOTIVES • 41

Corfe Common, Swanage Railway, Saturday, 13 May 2023: Class 33/0 D6515/33012 tails the Class 40 hauled 15.39 Swanage to River Frome.

Cowley Bridge Junction, Exeter, Monday, 27 July 1992: Class 33/0s 33025 *Sultan* and 33047 *Spitfire*, some distance from their Eastleigh base, with both in Civil Engineers' livery, approach the Junction with an early afternoon loaded ballast from Meldon Quarry.

seen down the branch from Okehampton and Meldon to Exeter Riverside yard. The Civil Engineers' 'Dutch' livery (so named because its yellow and grey resembled the colours used by Dutch Railways) was applied during the early 1990s. From Okehampton, the branch is single as far as Crediton, running alongside but not joining the Barnstaple branch from Coleford Junction (this is now only a nomenclature as no longer physically connected) until it reaches Crediton signal box. Thence there is double track for approximately a mile before it returns to single line until at Cowley Bridge Junction it joins the GWR Main Line.

Class 37

Class 37 locomotives were very well established around the traditional BR Scottish, Eastern, and Western (South Wales) regions, with occasional appearances in the North West, where their 1,750hp English Electric engines appealed to traffic managers for their reliability and impressive power. The Southern saw the occasional Class 37 in charge of Railfreight Petroleum Sector oil tank trains such as those from Ripple Lane to Horsham and to Portfield, Chichester. They also shared Southern tracks to and from Weymouth as far

Wandsworth Road, Wednesday, 3 April 1996: front: Class 37/7 37709 in Trainload Petroleum livery, second: Class 33/0 33065 *Sealion* in Civil Engineers' livery proceed in a light engine movement south, most likely from nearby Stewarts Lane depot, both in power. Note in the distance the curve to Nine Elms Junction for the Eurostar's access to Waterloo International. The recently renovated and redeveloped Battersea Power Station stands proud – a famed presence in many railway photographs taken here.

Ropley, Mid Hants Railway, Saturday, 27 April 2002: Class 37/0 37065 in Mainline Freight livery arrives with a late morning service from Alton bound for Alresford.

as Dorchester when diagrammed for working busier services originating at Bristol. During the Private Sector era, they were part of the DRS deployment of SERCo test and track-recording trains in the Central Division of the Southern Region. Class 37s also operated the Stockton to Sheerness scrap trains.

Class 37 37709 seen on page 42 was introduced to service in 1961 as D6714 and initially based at Stratford. January 1981 saw it transferred to Glasgow's Eastfield depot from where it worked diverse trains such as rush hour services to Dundee and West Highland line services to Oban and Mallaig. In March 1994 it was transferred to Stewarts Lane as one of the Class 37/7 fleet and allocated to Trainload Freight South, thus to Southern territory. 1997 saw it transferred to Eastleigh with its withdrawal in 2011.

New in November 1962, the above Class 37 was delivered as D6765 to Thornaby depot and spent most of its life in the north east, enjoying some summer seaside trips including Sheffield to Cleethorpes in August 1984, some Skegness to Grantham seaside trains in 1987. It spent time in 1991 with Railfreight Distribution at Tinsley depot, and in the summer of 1992 it was used on the Manchester Victoria to Blackpool 'Club' trains. Summer 1998 saw its use along the North Wales coast – another seaside opportunity. Still in service with BR, it saw a busy schedule operating as part of the Mid Hants Diesel gala in 2002, as seen here. It represents a class of locomotive which continued to appeal to privatised operators such as DRS, Colas and West Coast Railways well into the second decade of the twenty-first century. They continue to operate test trains on behalf of Network Rail, deploying Colas Class 37s.

Class 40

Class 40s may well have never appeared on the Southern Region but their ancestry is directly linked to the English Electric Bulleid prototype locomotives 10201-3, which were built for the Southern as main-line diesels. These had the same wheel arrangement, 1-Co-Co-1, as the Class 40 and also shared the same English Electric 16-cylinder engines. The first two locomotives, with a power unit of 1,750hp, were designed and built at Ashford (10201 in November 1950, 10202 in July 1951) and the third, equipped with a larger 2,000hp engine, at Brighton (10203 in March 1954). The LMR took possession of these trend-setting locomotives in 1955 and by 1957 they were returning approximately twice the annual mileage of similar powered express steam locomotives. This Class 40 carries the route code panel on the front rather than the front access doors which featured in the Pilot Scheme locomotives.

I recall seeing them in charge of container trains speeding through Rhyl en route to Holyhead and working parcels (including the famed Manchester Red Bank parcels trains) and oil tanker trains – clearly a versatile Class of locomotive. However, their troublesome train heating boilers and heavy weight in ratio to their power meant that their service life was inevitably shorter than with other Classes of locomotive introduced at later dates within the Modernisation Plan.

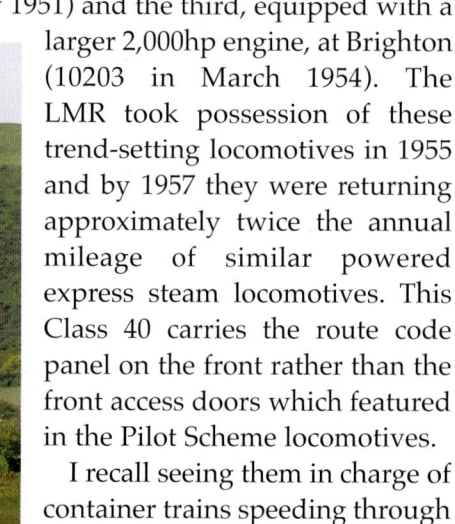

Corfe Common, Swanage Railway, Saturday, 13 May 2023: Class 40 40145 heads the 13.32 River Frome to Swanage.

Class 42

A product of Swindon Works, built in 1961, this 'Warship' Class locomotive was powered by diesel-hydraulic engines, two Maybach MD650s providing a power of 2,270hp in total, and Mekydro transmission. Such a design was based closely on the Deutsche Bundesbahn German B-B Class V200 which were also powered by Maybach engines. Seventy-one 'Warships' were built, with thirty-seven Class 42s constructed by Swindon with the aforementioned Maybach engines and thirty-three Class 43 manufactured by North British with MAN engines, excepting D830 which was equipped with Paxman engines when built by Swindon. They were based at several Western Region depots including Laira (Plymouth), Newton Abbot, Bristol Bath Road, Old Oak Common and in Wales at Cardiff, Swansea and Newport. Their main duties were found in their allocation to West of England main line expresses from Paddington to Bristol and the West Country, and in hauling inter-regional expresses between the north east and south west.

On Southern lines, they could be found working Exeter to Barnstaple and Ilfracombe services, sharing tracks from Dorchester with Bristol to Weymouth services and, from September 1964, they formed the main motive power on the London Waterloo to Exeter St Davids route. This was a result of the withdrawal of steam from such services and a strong inclination by the Southern to specify the Class owing to its perceived reliability and adequate power for the demanding gradients west of Salisbury. They initially operated from Newton Abbot depot but later shared depots with Plymouth Laira. The 10.12 Brighton to

Corfe Castle, Swanage Railway, Saturday, 8 May 2016: 'Warship' Class 42 D832 *Onslaught* makes a fine sight as it departs with the 10.45 Norden to Swanage.

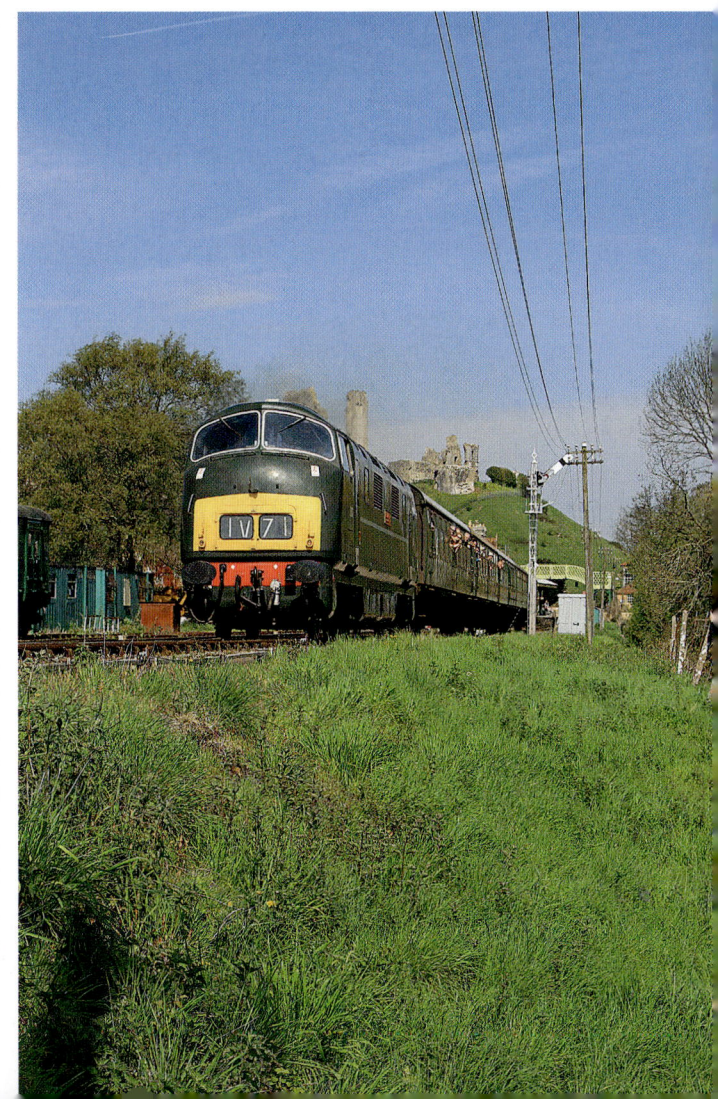

Plymouth and the 10.40 Plymouth to Brighton were Class 42 duties west of Salisbury. In 1966 BR decided, ill-advisedly as proved the case, to single long sections of the route west of Salisbury, and consequently train punctuality was essential in order for the single line to function properly. The Class 42s proved their worth in fulfilling this challenge. It was 1971 before the Class saw their final year in service along this route.

Class 44, 45 and 46

This was the famed D100, introduced in May 1961, when new to Derby, that great railway centre of the Midland Railway, with 1-Co-Co-1 wheel arrangement and withdrawn from service at the end of 1985. After Derby, it was then based at nearby Toton from March 1964, ending up at Cricklewood East in 1974 before returning to its original Toton base in 1976. It was renumbered 45060 in January 1975. Distinguished by its split headcode, it avoided the fate that other locomotives of the Class endured which were transitioned through a central headcode panel, which was already embodied in the later Class 46, before the majority received plated-over nose ends with sealed beam headlights in the 1970s. The Class wore BR lined green at first, followed by BR blue, some with small yellow panels, and ultimately the Class wore full yellow ends as carried here. During their final months

Corfe Common, Swanage Railway, Saturday, 9 May 2009: Class 45 45060 *Sherwood Forester*, preserved at Barrow Hill, departs Corfe Castle with the 11.50 Norden to Swanage.

in operation, a number of charters were run featuring visits to locations beyond their normal operations, when the 'Peak' Class was seen on Southern metals hauling such excursions as Pathfinder Tours' 'The Wessex Adventurer' in November 1988, which visited Southampton, Fawley and Weymouth. Bizarrely, the Peaks featured in the late 1960s and early 1970s on a scheduled summer Mondays / Wednesdays/Saturdays Motorail/Sleeper service from Newhaven Harbour to Stirling, routed via the West London Line and continuing along the GWR rather than West Coast Main Line.

Illustrating the central headcode fitted to the Class 46s referred to above, the immaculate BR blue certainly embellishes the locomotive's general appearance in recalling the BR blue era. The main issue with that livery was simply that *every* locomotive appeared in such a standardised livery, with very few exceptions permitted, and such has remained an issue for many nationalised railways – Germany with DB red, for example – and it is the privatisation era that has facilitated the wider application of some very attractive and eye-catching liveries both in the UK and in Europe.

D182 was constructed by BR Derby and delivered new in September 1962 and withdrawn in November 1984 from Gateshead depot, which had been its home depot throughout its career. It was one of the third batch of fifty-six of these Sulzer Type 4 locomotives built from 1961-63. It was powered by the same Sulzer 12-cylinder 12LDA28 as the Class 44 and 45s, producing 2,500hp, though with six Brush traction motors rather than the Crompton Parkinson traction motors provided in the Class 44 and 45. It would have regularly been seen operating

Corfe Common, Swanage Railway, Saturday, 7 May 2022: Class 46 D182/46045 heads the 17.15 Swanage to Corfe Castle.

Trans-Pennine expresses from Newcastle to Liverpool, and along the East Coast Main Line.

Fortunate photographers at this location on this occasion merely needed to cross the bridge in order to see one of the ten Class 44s at the back of the same train seen in the previous photograph. It offers a useful opportunity to compare and contrast these veteran Class partners. D4 was constructed by BR Derby and introduced to service in September 1959; it was withdrawn from Toton depot in November 1980. It shared the Sulzer 12-cylinder 12LDA28 power unit with the later built Class 44 and 45 locomotives, although their version was an up-rated one. They were distinguished by their being named after famous Peaks which featured along the routes that the Peak Class plied. For this reason, these were really the only true 'Peaks' but the term has been acknowledged in common use for the Class 44, 45 and 46. Their front design incorporated a central two-door gangway connection in the nose end and they carried the disc and lamp headcodes which are reminiscent of those we saw on the Class 26 and 27s. They spent much of their lives on the Midland Main Line and they must have been impressive locomotives to experience climbing through the Peak district en route from Manchester to St Pancras. Unfortunately, a number of problems

Corfe Common, Swanage Railway, Saturday, 7 May 2022: Class 44 D4/44004 *Great Gable* tails the 17.15 Swanage to Corfe Castle.

arose during their service, especially with their steam generators and traction motor and main generator flashovers.

This short collection of photographs amply illustrates their appeal in preservation. I recall seeing and being hauled by them on the Trans-Pennine services to and from Liverpool and the North Wales Coast, and not forgetting forging their way along the challenging Settle and Carlisle whereon rugged locomotives met rugged wilderness in all seasons.

45108 was one of the Class 45s originally fitted with central nose-end headcode

Right and below: In the first picture we see passing Corfe Common, Swanage Railway, Saturday, 13 May 2023: Class 45 D120/45108 at the rear of the 13.39 service from Swanage to Norden. In the second picture approaching Harmans Cross, Saturday, 7 May 2022, we see Class 46 D182/46045 heading the 15.39 Corfe Castle to Swanage.

boxes, which were formed of two separate windows, each covering two digits. One intriguing link between the Peaks and the Class 47 locomotives is that Crewe-built Class 45 D57 received a 12LDA28-C engine as fitted to the Class 47s, although within a relatively short time this was replaced by the same engine as its peers, mainly as a result of there being a shortage of qualified drivers.

At their scheduled classified repairs from 1973 onwards the Class 45s either had just their airbrake installations completed with the steam generators retained, or rebuilt to one of the fifty Class 45/1s with electric train heating (ETH). Such required the boiler to be removed and fitting with an electrical control cubicle containing the ETH control and switchgear supplied by Brush. The Class 45s formed the main motive power for the Midland Division for over twenty years, replaced by the HSTs for the Cross Country routes and the St Pancras services.

Class 47
In the 1980s, 47702 *Saint Cuthbert* would have been seen in charge of Glasgow to Aberdeen, Edinburgh and Inverness InterCity services, previously having been part of the Class 47/4 fleet as 47504, in BR blue livery, until as part of a batch of 47/4s it was rebuilt at BREL Crewe in 1979, which saw seventeen of the Class modified with push-pull equipment for use on high speed services between Edinburgh and Glasgow. With 2,580hp available from the Sulzer 12 LDA28C engines and Brush TM172 generator, it would have been well equipped for the Scottish main lines and terrain. With the arrival of the era of Network SouthEast, the locomotive was bestowed with the house colours of red, blue, white and grey when it moved south in 1990 for service with Network SouthEast. Consequently, it was based at Old Oak Common – a Western Region depot – while rostered for working the London to Salisbury and Exeter services. It is clear from reports by railway managers at the time that the photograph of this locomotive on page 51 was taken that the Class 47s and rolling stock used on the route from Waterloo to Exeter were becoming tired and run down, with little time or opportunity to remedy technical problems and give some train care to the carriages either at their servicing depots of Old Oak Common or Laira, as the diagrams for their use were tight and allowed little flexibility.

The Class 47/4 will have arrived on an earlier service from the South West although at this stage, the Parcels Sector Class 47/4s were not allocated any passenger duties.

DIESEL AND ELECTRIC LOCOMOTIVES • 51

London Waterloo, Saturday, 27 February 1993. Left: Class 47/7 47702 *Saint Cuthbert* in NSE livery has arrived on the 06.45 from Exeter St Davids, with Network SouthEast and Regional Railways liveries in the carriage formation. Right: Class 47/4 47489 *Crewe Diesel Depot* in Parcels livery, at the buffers, light engine.

Orpington, Tuesday, 31 May 1988: Class 47 47152 with a northbound mixed freight.

This train may well have originated in Dover, as the chemical tankers may have come over on the train ferry, and it is highly likely to use the West London line to reach Willesden Yard for sorting and forwarding to other parts of the country. The ubiquitous Class 47s stretched their legs from the far north to the far south of the UK in the 1980s and early '90s, including Kent and East Sussex. They featured on parcels trains from Dover to Newcastle and from Redhill to Swindon, from Tonbridge to London Bridge, Preston and Glasgow, also on trip freights and ferry van workings from Dover to London's marshalling yards and Severn Tunnel Junction, especially when carrying imported fruit and vegetables. They were in charge of InterCity services from Manchester to Dover, Glasgow to Ramsgate and Glasgow to Brighton (the latter routed via Kensington Olympia and East Croydon though occasionally diverted owing to Sunday engineering via Redhill and Guildford as far as Reading). They also featured on InterCity services from Dover Western Docks to Liverpool Lime Street, and from Folkestone to Wolverhampton and Manchester. An especially noteworthy working was the Travelling Post Office from Dover to Norwich. They achieved some additional status when allocated to the Gypsum trains from Mountfield to Northfleet Cement Works. The Class 47s' involvement in the movement of aggregates saw a significant upturn when the Thamesport facility on the Isle of Grain opened. They were also well established with the ARC (Amey Roadstone Corporation) hopper trains working from Allington to Westbury.

The eye-catching Rail Express Systems livery with horizontal blue bands and graphite grey applied to the top third of the locomotive incorporated the Post Office colours of Royal Mail red; the parcels carrying operations of British Rail became Rail Express Systems (RES) in 1991. Royal Mail and parcels traffic came under the RES banner as did the conversion of stock to roller-shutter doors. The first of the Class 47/7s to wear the livery was 47774, which it carried from 1993.This sub-Class was modified with long-range fuel tanks and had jumper cables mounted on the cab ends which enabled them to work with Propelling Control Vehicles (PCVs) on mail train services emanating from the new Willesden Railnet terminal. No doubt 47757 has just come off RES-related duties on the Southern. Parcels operations on the Southern in the early 1980s would have passed through Kensington Olympia on the West London line, with workings to/from Clapham Junction, Dover, East Croydon, Redhill and Three Bridges serving a diverse network as far away as Birkenhead and the Midlands.

DIESEL AND ELECTRIC LOCOMOTIVES • 53

Redhill, Friday, 26 July 1996: RES Class 47/7 47757 *Restitution* arrives from the Reigate direction.

'The Pines Express' was an established named train, recalling the pine trees prevalent in south Dorset, which took eager holiday makers to the South Coast resort of Bournemouth, 'The Centre of Health and Pleasure' as one LMS poster declared. It was a direct service linking Manchester and Bournemouth although it originally ran via Bath Green Park, Shepton Mallet and Evercreech Junction along the famed Somerset and Dorset Railway. It provided a convenient way for families to reach the south coast in an age when

Eastleigh, Saturday, 16 October 1999: Virgin Cross Country Trains Class 47/4 in Virgin livery and with accompanying Virgin Trains livery coaching set passes with the 08.17 Manchester Piccadilly to Bournemouth *'The Pines Express'.*

Bincombe Tunnel (south portal), Saturday, 25 October 1986: Class 47/3 47362 emerges with a Weymouth-bound train consist of Civil Engineers and Railfreight wagons including a couple of Speedlink wagons.

car ownership was relatively uncommon. The Midland Railway was delighted to provide passengers from the Midlands and Yorkshire with direct trains which used the route to reach LSWR metals for the final few miles to the resort. When Beeching's axe saw closure in 1966 of the Somerset and Dorset Railway, these trains were diverted to the south west main line via Reading and Southampton.

It would be May 1988 before the third rail seen ready in place for the Bournemouth to Weymouth electrification would see implementation of electric trains. This Class 47 was built as D1881 in 1965. It was one of a sub-class which were not fitted with train heating. Their generator was of the Brush type TM172 in comparison to the Class 47/0 and 47/2s which were fitted with the Brush type TG160. It was finally withdrawn in 1998 whilst allocated to Bescot depot. When kept clean, the Railfreight grey livery with wrap-around yellow cabs and large logo looked quite smart and was no doubt utilitarian in being easier to camouflage the everyday grime that builds up on any stock travelling around the rails of the UK.

Extraordinarily, a summer Okehampton car carrier service operated from Exeter St Davids from June 1960 until September 1964 using converted GUVs and three passenger coaches. The revival of the Okehampton branch to regular passenger trains in November 2021 is truly one of the most positive rail re-openings in recent history, with hourly services from May 2022 resulting in consistently well patronised trains maintained throughout the day as well as in the rush-hours. Given a realistic project set in place and funding approved, helped by a pre-existing route already in place (one that had been protected from intrusive housing or agricultural development), railways closed in the past can be successfully reinstated and an appropriate level of service provided to encourage use by those living within reach of stations involved.

After the reopening, further work was carried out to the Okehampton station buildings which have been restored fully intact and in their original architectural style. This was honoured to the extent that genuine Southern Railway green colours were used with great care taken to keep to as close a paint match as possible, all thanks to efforts of Dartmoor Railway Association and Devon County Council. Although the station is unstaffed, with a vending machine supplying tickets, the building incorporates toilets, a heritage-style waiting room, a shop for the Dartmoor Railway Association and a Dartmoor National Park Information centre

Okehampton, Dartmoor Railway, Sunday, 10 April 2005: Class 47/7 47716, previously 47507, in Rail Express Systems livery and then preserved on the Dartmoor Railway, at the rear of the 14.30 Okehampton to Sampford Courtenay. The stock includes two Mk. II First Class carriages, a Trailer Buffet and an ex-parcels generator van.

and a cafe. The former booking office has also been restored to its former glory, with period posters and signage helping to add to the atmosphere of this once Southern Railway outpost. Encouragingly, twice the number of passengers originally forecast now use the reopened line.

This is a busy scene for what was historically a quiet LSWR branch line station, with most passengers passing through to the seaside resort of Swanage. In contrast, an intense service featuring preserved diesels at a spring gala brings much attention from photographers and enthusiasts keen on travelling behind as many locomotives as they can.

47635, built at Crewe as D1606, was delivered new in 1964 and withdrawn in March 2004. The headcode panel was no longer needed for displaying the four character train reporting number after such was deemed unnecessary after 1976, and initially these panels would simply show four zeros. This locomotive shows the

Corfe Castle Station, Swanage Railway, Sunday, 11 May 2008: Right: Class 47/4 47635 *The Lass O' Ballochmyle*, then preserved on the Swanage Railway, is hauling the 16.30 Swanage to Norden. Left: Class 20 20096, in Railfreight Metals and Automotive decals, leads the 16.50 Norden to Harmans Cross. In the far right, stabled in the Up siding, can be seen Class 117 Pressed Steel Suburban 3-car DMU (51346, 51388, 59516).

DIESEL AND ELECTRIC LOCOMOTIVES • 57

following stage when the headcode box received black plastic film and two white dots. Such is seen in the second picture with 47635 showing this headcode box style with its accompanying large logo blue livery. As 47029 it was allocated to the Western Region, and in the late 1970s and early 1980s was shedded at Laira, Cardiff and Bristol depots. It was transferred to the Scottish Region when in 1986 as 47635 it was based at Edinburgh and later at Inverness depots.

The two-tone green of the 1960s British Railways era seems to have been particularly popular as the livery has been favoured for several of the preserved members of the Class 47s, and it looks particularly interesting when contrasted with the Metropolitan red carried by the 4TC push-pull 4-carriage set, courtesy of London Transport, which operated between London and Swanage from 1967 to 1969 and on the main line between London and Weymouth from 1967 to 1988 when the Bournemouth to Weymouth line was electrified. Eight carriages were selected and extracted from six 4TC sets to form two complete units which were purchased by London Underground in 1992. Bars were fitted over the drop lights, clearly

Corfe Common, Swanage Railway, Sunday, 11 May 2008: Class 47/4 47635 *The Lass O' Ballochmyle* is seen hauling the 14.10 Norden to Harmans Cross.

Harmans Cross, Swanage Railway, Saturday, 13 May 2023: Class 47/4 D1645/47830 makes an impressive sweep away from Harmans Cross with the 15.15 Swanage to Corfe Castle.

evident here, and repainted into Metropolitan red and brown livery, with mauve and blue lining and gold numbering; these were then used for excursions on the LT surface lines.

Class 50

Seaton Junction station may have closed in March 1966, but there are still traces of Southern green on the remaining canopies. One of the most significant developments in the era of the Southern during the late 1980s and early 1990s was the Network SouthEast revolution. It was thanks to the vision of an enterprising, charismatic and radical senior railway manager, Chris Green, who launched the concept of 'Network SouthEast,' previously known as the London and South East sector, and this did much to revolutionise travel within the South East, incorporating the full network of the Southern Region as far as Exeter. Accompanying the initiative was the launch of a bright and colourful livery applied to locomotives and multiple units (diesel and electric), and an aggressive marketing drive to encourage public use of over 8,000 trains on 27 routes over

2,500 route miles of railways. The train fleets were refurbished, their interior cleanliness prioritised, stations spruced up and amenities improved, and off-peak services increased. Regional railway branding for the Southern was launched such as 'Kent Link', 'South London Lines', 'Island Line' (Isle of Wight), 'Wessex Electrics', and 'SouthWestern Lines'. Route Managers worked with close teams devolved from local managers. The great complex of the Southern network would become 'customer friendly'. Stations displayed the Network SouthEast map just to keep the profile of the endeavour in the eye of the travelling public.

While I observed much of the Network SouthEast revolution from the distant West Country, its impact was still unavoidable as demonstrated when the consequences of such colossal change saw Class 50s forming empty coach stock workings clambering up Hemerdon incline following their servicing at Laira or 47/7s turning up at Plymouth with full rakes of coaches on the Sundays 14.55 Plymouth to London Waterloo, all in Network SouthEast livery.

Seaton Junction, Saturday, 22 July 1989: Class 50 50050 *Fearless*, in Network SouthEast livery, passes at speed with the 17.15 London Waterloo to Exeter St Davids.

Occasional 'Network SouthEast Days' (inevitably on Saturdays – thereby facilitating use of stock otherwise not required off peak) offered me opportunities to travel up from the south west, using the exceptionally low price flat fare tickets allowing unlimited travel anywhere in the Network SouthEast territory, either behind a Class 50, 47/7 or a hard-working Class 33. I would then explore the multitudinous branches and sections of main line offered by the plethora of lines within the Southern travel area.

This Class 50 was withdrawn in December 1990 after suffering power unit damage after providing twenty-two years of service, having been introduced in July 1968. It narrowly

Left: **Corfe Common**, Swanage Railway, Saturday, 7 May 2022: Class 50 50026 *Indomitable* heads the 12.39 Corfe Castle to Swanage.

Below: **Harman's Cross**, Swanage Railway, Saturday, 7 May 2022: Class 50 50026 *Indomitable* approaches with the 15.32 River Frome to Swanage.

DIESEL AND ELECTRIC LOCOMOTIVES • 61

avoided the cutter's torch after spending some time at a scrap yard in Rotherham. As D426 in BR blue livery – one that suited the Class 50s' long body profile particularly well – it would have been seen working express trains along the West Coast Main Line from Preston to Glasgow either singly or double-headed with a fellow Class 50. Two Class 50s, 50023 *Howe* and 50017 *Royal Oak*, were painted in Network SouthEast livery especially to coincide with the launch day of Network SouthEast, 10 June 1986. In total, twenty-nine of the Class 50s were painted into Network SouthEast livery. 50026 here carries a later revised version of the Network SouthEast livery in which the red and white body stripes continue to the end of the cabs with blue cab window surrounds.

There is no question that the Class 50s in preservation have received a dedicated and enthusiastic following, helped by the coordinated efforts of the Class 50 Alliance Ltd. which maintains six Class 50s, 50007 *Hercules*, 50031 *Hood*, 50033 *Glorious*, 50035 *Ark Royal*, 50044 *Exeter* and 50049 *Defiance*, all of which are based at the Severn Valley Railway and three of which – 50007, 50044 and 50049 – are main line registered for use on Network Rail's infrastructure. The Fifty Fund is a society which helps to promote the activity of the Class 50 Alliance by raising money to fund its preservation activities. They provide illustrated presentations to railway societies. Former Laira depot Fleet Manager Geoff Hudson has put together a fascinating tribute to the Class 50s from their

Corfe Common, Swanage Railway, Saturday, 12 May 2012: Class 50 50026 *Indomitable* heads the 17.05 Norden to Harmans Cross.

inception through to their final years with British Railways and their consequent life in preservation.

Demonstrating the Class 50s' popularity to photographers, the weight limit of the small overbridge crossing the Barnstaple branch line at this quiet request halt was substantially tested to its limit on this occasion with a large number of camera and video-wielding enthusiasts keen to capture their passing in the pleasant spring lighting.

It is worth noting that through trains and portions from Waterloo to North Devon and Cornwall ceased after the 1964 summer season, although one holiday service operated in summer 1965 from Paddington via Yeovil Junction to Bude and Ilfracombe on Saturdays only, although this service was diverted to run via Taunton the following year. Motive power was usually a Class 42 Warship.

Cascaded Class 50s, displaced by the introduction of the HSTs on the West Country main line, were provided for the Waterloo to

Newton St Cyres, Saturday, 26 March 2022: Class 50 Operations locomotives
Class 50 Alliance-owned Class 50 50007 *Hercules*, in GBRf livery, leads UK Railtours' 'Springtime Hoovering' excursion from London Paddington to Paignton and Okehampton. This was the Paignton to Okehampton leg of the tour. The excursion name is a double entendre, Springtime cleaning often involves hoovering up the dust and cobwebs, and the locomotives' favoured name among their aficionados is 'Hoovers' after their distinctive sound produced by the dynamic braking resistor cooling fan.

DIESEL AND ELECTRIC LOCOMOTIVES • 63

Approaching Cowley Bridge, Saturday, 26 March 2022: Class 50 Operations locomotives Class 50 Alliance-owned Class 50 50007 *Hercules* (posing as 50034), in GBRf livery, tails the return Okehampton to Exeter St Davids section of the UK Railtours' 'Springtime Hoovering' excursion from London Paddington to Paignton and Okehampton. 50049 *Defiance* is the leading locomotive.

Exeter main line from May 1980 following a period of familiarisation at Salisbury and Waterloo train crew depots. They were seen as the optimum solution to replace the over-stretched Class 33s at the time, especially in view of the fact that the six basic locomotive diagrams were amongst the highest mileage duties in the country with a daily mileage that exceeded the fuel range of most Classes of diesel at that time. The Class 50s' longer range fuel tanks could solve such a problem and with their 100mph capability they could achieve a higher speed as far as Basingstoke – thanks also to improved train pathing between electric services on the Bournemouth main line. In May 1982 the number of Class 50 turns was increased to seven with the addition of an extra Mk II coaching set, thus permitting an hourly service.

There was increasing concern by Southern Region managers that the use of the heavy Class 50s (117 tons) had an adverse effect on the track condition, and indeed the demanding stop-start service pattern with many stations en-route and track condition on the heavily used sections towards Waterloo began to cause fatigue failures on underframe engine mountings. Maintenance costs increased accompanied by rectification of associated problems. Service reliability became depressingly low. In 1987, the introduction of sectorisation of resources meant that the Exeter to Waterloo route came under Network SouthEast, and subsequently brand-named the 'West of England'. Remaining work on carriages at Clapham Junction was transferred to Eastleigh and later to Plymouth Laira depot. This resulted in a higher profile being given to addressing the challenges posed by both the route and the use of Class 50s, their power unit overhauls having been transferred to Crewe from Doncaster. Network SouthEast would now sponsor maintenance of the Class 50s.

Class 55
'A Deltic on the Southern?' you may ask with raised eyebrows. Ah yes, but it did happen. The type was withdrawn from BR service in 1982. However, this Deltic, 55022 *Royal Scots Grey*, did indeed feature weekly hauling Virgin Trains operated summer Saturday scheduled services from Birmingham to Ramsgate in 1998 and 1999.This was at a time when Deltic 9000 Locomotives Limited had charge of the locomotive. In 1998, the Deltic was scheduled to haul the 06.58 Birmingham to Ramsgate, returning on the 11.26 Ramsgate to Edinburgh as far as Birmingham between 30 May and 26 September. In spring 1999, Virgin confirmed that for the Summer Saturdays season, D9000 would be the booked locomotive. The reason behind this special hire was not so much to fill the service with rail enthusiasts who would not otherwise be travelling as patrons of Virgin Trains but rather because there was a lack of appropriate motive power available for express passenger trains such as the Birmingham to Ramsgate Cross Country service. There was even talk of additional preserved Deltics being revived for an expansion in such duties, but that was probably over-optimistic in view of the fact that the Birmingham to Ramsgate Summer Saturdays service no longer ran in 2000.

DIESEL AND ELECTRIC LOCOMOTIVES • 65

Corfe Castle, Swanage Railway, Saturday, 9 May 2009: 'Deltic' Class 55 55022 *Royal Scots Grey* hauls the 10.10 Norden to Harmans Cross. Class 31 31108 is at the rear. Class 117 Pressed Steel DMU DMBS 51346 and DMS 51388, preserved at the Swanage Railway, are within the train consist at the rear of the coaching set. In the distance, Class 26 26007 departs Corfe Castle station at the rear of the 10.04 Harmans Cross to Norden.

Deltics certainly look powerful and exude a presence matched by their two Napier Deltic engines which hum loudly when accelerating away from stations or climbing gradients gracefully and majestically. Their appeal is enhanced by the fact that only twenty-two were built and they established a reputation for reliability and strength as they were timetabled to take advantage of their 100mph capability where long stretches of the East Coast Main Line favoured high speed. London King's Cross to Edinburgh was also a prestigious route and one that required a locomotive design capable of living up to the accompanying high expectations of them. Doncaster Works could efficiently carry out

Above and right:
In the first picture, at Corfe Common, Swanage Railway, Saturday, 9 May 2009,'Deltic' Class 55 55022 *Royal Scots Grey* is seen in charge of the 13.50 Norden to Swanage.
In the second picture, the same locomotive is seen later approaching Harmans Cross with the 15.10 Swanage to Norden.

DIESEL AND ELECTRIC LOCOMOTIVES • 67

specialist repairs and engine changes, their dedication ensuring that the locomotives' performance was consistent with maximised output and efficiency.

Class 56

The Class 56 locomotives were initially essentially dedicated to merry-go-round coal trains working between the National Coal Board collieries and the power stations of the Central Electricity Generating Board. Consequently, their main duties were in the North East, Yorkshire and Nottinghamshire. However, they later spread their wings to haul heavy stone trains such as seen here, and for this purpose some were based at Westbury. Their appearance on the Southern must have proved a welcome sight when the main rail traffic to be seen was a plethora of EMUs. They could be seen hauling coal trains from Welbeck Colliery to the Northfleet Cement terminal in Kent, routed via Kew, Lewisham and the Dartford Loop. They could also be seen hauling the Coatbridge to Southampton Freightliners. They often took charge of aggregates trains to and from Maidstone, and eight Class 56s were allocated to Hither Green in October 1990 replacing re-deployed Class 60s coming in to service. They consequently acquired diagrams for

Redhill, Saturday, 24 October 1987: Class 56 56048 with empty ARC wagons returning west via Reading, probably bound for the ARC Whatley Quarry at Frome or Tytherington Quarry. At platform the 14.05 to Tonbridge, formed of a Class 119 Gloucester RCW DMU, awaits at platform.

the Trainload Construction Sector, providing special interest when working from Cliffe to Purley. The short-lived Fastline freight subsidiary saw two Class 56s dedicated to a container service from Doncaster to Thamesport, returning from Grain overnight. The Tytherington Quarry trains were routed via the North Kent Line from Allington sidings.

Class 57/3
The Class 57/3s were re-engineered from Class 47s, in the case of 57312 from 47330/D1811. They were fitted with a refurbished EMD engine and a reconditioned alternator. This improved their reliability and performance. When the Class 57/3 locomotives were originally converted, the Virgin Class 57/3s retained conventional draw gear. It was decided that some sort of auto coupler was needed; consequently, Brush Traction designed a complex and somewhat unsightly auto drop-head Dellner coupler to facilitate attaching the locomotive to a Pendolino coupling and to help with onboard train power. Eventually all of the Class 57/3s were retro

Corfe Common, Swanage Railway, Saturday, 12 May 2012: Network Rail Class 57/3 57312, based at Eastleigh Works, with Class 73 73 136 *Perseverance* immediately behind, passes with the 18.10 Norden to Swanage. BR Class 4MT 2-6-4T 80104 assists from the rear. Class 73 73136 was added at short notice to this diesel gala, as it was required for acting as a brake translator for the Class 57/3.

fitted with such. In Network Rail's bright yellow livery 57312, now owned by the Rail Operations Group, certainly complements the yellow fields of rapeseed in the background.

Class 58

Here's another Class of locomotive which in its BR years fulfilled its main purpose of providing traction for the merry-go-round traffic between collieries and power stations, just as the Class 56s successfully fulfilled. All of the fleet was allocated to the Trainload Coal Sector and based at Toton. In November 1994 the Class was rebadged as part of 'Mainline Freight', when British Rail decided to concentrate its freight operations in three 'shadow freight' companies with Mainline in charge of freight logistics operations to the south and east, extending from South Yorkshire to Kent. On the Southern, the Class 58s saw use with the merry-go-round coal trains to Northfleet and Ridham Dock, and in Sheerness Steel diagrams. By the mid-nineties their freight-hauling scope had been broadened and workings such as aggregate and oil were as frequent for the class as diagrammed coal workings such as the Chessington coal trains. To facilitate this broader range of traffic in the Southern area, several Class 58s were often out-based at Eastleigh, Hither Green and Stewarts Lane. Their work on aggregates trains to and from the

Clapham Junction, Wednesday, 3 April 1996: Class 58 58027 in Trainload Mainline Freight livery passes with a Bardon stone train from Angerstein Wharf bound for Thorney Mill Stone Discharge Terminal.

East Midlands 'such as seen here' took the Class to new locations including Barnham and Angerstein Wharf. They also featured with LPG trains from Furzebrook to Hallen Marsh.

Class 66

This appealing station lies between Kew Bridge and Barnes Bridge stations and is served by South Western Trains. It lay on the branch line of the LSWR from Windsor to Waterloo and opened in 1849 on the Windsor, Staines and South Western Railway. The Station House was built by William Tite in the style of a classical villa and is Grade II listed. The refreshed stonework of the historical building contrasts with the grime acquired by a standard Class 66 workhorse of the modern traction scene. No doubt that with the increased traffic produced by the HS2 construction project underway there is little turn-around time for the locomotive to receive a much-needed clean, and such is consequently of a lower priority than getting on with the job of moving the materials needed to help provide the construction to keep apace. GBRf's willingness to embrace new markets and opportunities has been rewarded with consequent remarkable success.

Steady increases in aggregates traffic from the late 1990s onwards have proved particularly rewarding for the new railfreight

Chiswick, Saturday, 11 March 2023: GBRf Class 66/7 66740 passes with the 08.55 West Ruislip to Grain container flats which had carried concrete lining segment rings for the HS2 tunnels under construction.

Clapham Junction, Tuesday, 26 May 2009: Right: E.W.S. Class 66 66040 heads a southbound sand/aggregates train for Purley aggregates depot, early afternoon. Centre: South West Trains Class 455/9 5916 operating a London Waterloo to Dorking via Epsom early p.m. service.

companies which have offered increasingly competitive haulage rates when compared to road. Some existing terminals have been expanded, mothballed terminals reactivated and several new unloading points opened to accommodate the many new services. Creating paths for these freights must be an interesting occupation, especially where fitting them into already busy suburban passenger routes at complex interchange points such as Clapham Junction. If a freight train runs late as a result of the operator's reasons, then compensation is payable to the operators of the passenger and freight trains consequently delayed, and likewise if a late running passenger train delays a freight train which is running on time, then compensation is due to the operating company.

Freight train photographers can happily spend an hour here or line-siding somewhere on the Southampton to Oxford route in order to see a wide selection of trains on weekdays, mostly but not exclusively container traffic. A glance at the favoured website at Real Time Trains provides a commentary on which traffic might be expected to pass on any given day. Trains emanate from/to Southampton Western Docks from/to Masborough, West Yorkshire, Doncaster, Ditton, Hams Hall, East Midlands Gateway Terminal or Wakefield Europort. Southampton Container Terminal container trains head for Trafford Park Euro Terminal and Leeds Freightliner

Basingstoke, Thursday, 31 July 2014: Freightliner Class 66/5 66543 heads north with an early afternoon unidentified container train.

Terminal, while trains from Morris Cowley and Halewood (Jaguar cars) head for Southampton Eastern Docks. Then there is the Eastleigh to Cliffe Hill, and Eastleigh to Hinksey sidings Civil Engineers' trains. A Merehead Quarry to Woking service will provide an interesting alternative in terms of type of freight.

Favoured motive power seen in charge of these trains is the General Motors built Class 66 which became the established workhorse for the increased freight that came with railfreight privatisation. By spring 2016, a total of 485 had been supplied to the various operators including Freightliner's Class 66/6 locomotives delivered between 2000 and 2007 – these were equipped with a lower gear ratio and therefore higher tractive effort in comparison to the other Class 66s.

Some 5 million tonnes of aggregates and 600,000 tonnes of cement are moved annually by GBRf. The company has been able to supply traction for moving train loads from quarries and receiving terminals, replacing many thousands of lorry movements which would otherwise have cluttered up the nation's highways. Hanson Cement is one such example, with their trains operated between Ketton and Ribblesdale, Clitheroe. Tarmac is another customer benefiting from long-term contracts alongside those for moving stone from Peak District Quarries and, as seen above, moving train loads associated with HS2. Maritime Transport is a provider of

DIESEL AND ELECTRIC LOCOMOTIVES • 73

Tonbridge, Friday, 13 October 2023: GBRf Class 66/7 66727 *Maritime One* in Maritime livery arrives light engine from Dagenham Dock and awaits movement onto Tonbridge West Yard for stabling.

supply chain services, such as warehousing, railport services and container transport. Rival operator DB Cargo has painted seven of its Class 66/0s into a similar livery, all gaining the name 'Maritime Intermodal'.

Admittedly that which we see in the picture below is an unlikely pairing, with a modern freight locomotive and a slam-door EMU from the late 1960s and 1970s in harness, the two contrasting blue liveries carried by the locomotive and electric multiple unit (EMU) represent the different generations of rail blue, with the lighter blue of the 4-VEP reminding us of the standard BR blue hue and

Corfe Common, Swanage Railway, Sunday, 11 May 2008: GBRf Class 66/7 66724 *Drax Power Station*, delivered new January 2007, is seen hauling the 13.50 Norden to Swanage, formed of Class 423 4-Vep 3417 in BR blue, owned and restored by South West Trains for the latter days of slam-door workings.

the Privatisation company's blue as selected by GBRf featuring a common choice of blue, a variant of which is also seen in the previous photograph. Colourful liveries convey value just as 'Southern green' became synonymous with the Southern Railway and once was applied wholesale to the Southern Region's electric units.

Class 71

This Class was designed for mixed traffic use on the Southern Region; twenty-four were built in 1958 at Doncaster and introduced to service 1959-60. Renowned for their impressive acceleration and capable of 90mph, they saw use on the Southern's most prestigious services including the London Victoria to Paris *Golden Arrow/ Flèche d'Or* and *Night Ferry* trains as far as Dover, the former going forward in France via Calais Maritime, and the latter via Dunkirk. During the steam era, the train saw haulage by 'Battle of Britain' Class light Pacifics and by Britannia Class locomotives, as well as 'Merchant Navy' locomotives such as preserved 35028 *Clan Line*. These conveyed the famed Pullman carriages which featured as an integral part of such a renowned train. The *Golden Arrow* ran from 1929–72 with its final run on 30 September 1972.

Services which the Class 71 operated also included the *'Night Ferry'* passenger service and the South Eastern Travelling Post

London Waterloo, Saturday, 1 October 1988: Class 71 E5001 (71001), preserved as part of the National Collection at the NRM, is seen on display.

Office which operated between Dover and London Bridge until 1968, later to London Victoria until that service was withdrawn in February 1977. They also operated mixed loco-hauled van and passenger formations overnight, such as the 03.00 mixed parcels from London Victoria to Dover. In their early days they also sometimes saw use on Newhaven boat trains. Class 71s could be frequently seen along the South Eastern section of the Kent main line, in charge of continental ferry wagons between Dover docks and the London distribution terminal near Hither Green.

The Class 71s collected power from the third rail at between 660-750V dc. The centrally-mounted roof-pantograph was provided for use in yards where a live rail could not be expedited owing to safety reasons. Ten Class 71s were withdrawn for conversion into Class 74 electro-diesels. Eastleigh was fully occupied building new EMUs so these conversions took place at Crewe in 1967 and 1968, providing a bizarre sight of these purely Southern Region third rail locomotives being seen alongside LMR overhead electric Class 86s, being constructed for the West Coast Main Line, and Class 76s (in use on the Woodhead route) under heavy maintenance. These Class 74s worked the heavier boat trains into Southampton Docks and duties along the newly electrified Bournemouth line, and appropriately were based at Eastleigh. Some are reported as having worked down the Swanage branch with through trains from London Waterloo. The Class was entirely withdrawn by November 1977 when more reliable Class 73s became available.

Class 73 Electro-Diesel

Wearing the standard Gatwick Express livery, the Class 73/1s were placed in charge of the new 'Gatwick Express' services from their introduction in May 1984. 73123 was named 'Gatwick Express' and especially liveried by Stewarts Lane depot in the new two-tone grey, a waist height band of red and white, wrap-around yellow ends and an off-white roof. It also carried the large logo BR emblem. This new livery was received very well and the rest of the Class 73/1s were repainted in similar colours. The Class 73/2s were provided with an InterCity Swallow style livery to mark the emergence of Gatwick Express as a self-contained business in October 1993, thus reflecting the previous joint operation between Gatwick Express and InterCity Anglia, although this was subsequently modified by the removal of the InterCity logo which was replaced by the Gatwick Express logo and a maroon rather than red bodyside band.

76 • DIESEL AND ELECTRIC MOTIVE POWER ON THE SOUTHERN 1980s TO PRESENT

East Croydon, Saturday, 18 June 1994: Class 73/2 73207 *County of East Sussex* in Gatwick Express/InterCity livery passes with the 11.00 London Victoria to Gatwick. Note the variety of new and old livery in the carriage formation.

The carriage fleet was similarly re-liveried, that transition from old to new clearly evident here.

The large bodyside logo of 73006 is rather incongruous with the locomotive's height and length. However, the wrap around yellow cabsides may contribute to this as they 'shorten' the appearance of the true length of the locomotive. Some enthusiasts would prefer the BR Southern Region carriage green worn by 73006, as delivered numbered E6006 in November 1962. With light grey window

Woking, Saturday, 28 May 1988: to the right, Class 73/0 73006 and an unidentified Class 33 in blue livery are both stabled, while Class 33/0 33008 *Eastleigh* passes through light engine.

DIESEL AND ELECTRIC LOCOMOTIVES • 77

surrounds, a dark grey roof and red buffer beams, and bearing the lion and wheel BR emblem, the first batch of six locomotives – designed at Brighton but constructed at Eastleigh – looked very smart and almost debonair. Interestingly the very first of the Class 73s, E6001/73001, was delivered with small yellow warning panels on both cab ends. The second batch, or production fleet, of Class 73s were painted in BR Electric Blue.

It is worth noting that some of the design features of the Class 33 'Cromptons' were incorporated in the Class 73 design, such as the electric output of 1,600hp thus similar to the 1,550hp of the Class 33. Their long slab side appearance helped to increase their route availability, thereby allowing them access to the narrower Hastings gauge.

Here's another livery, two tone grey, which with the departmental grey worn by some of the Class, did not really enhance the elongated slab side of the Class 73s. Note the central headlight and the roof-mounted aerial for the cab radio equipment. The Class was equipped with air brakes and vacuum brakes accompanied by an additional electro-pneumatic system, all of which enabled these locomotives to work with a variety of 1950s and '60s EMUs. Electric train heating was available at all times but if the locomotive

Corfe Castle Station, Swanage Railway, Sunday, 11 May 2008: Class 73/1 73107 *Spitfire*, operated by GBRF Eastleigh, departs with the 17.05 Harmans Cross to Norden. At distant right, a Class 117 Pressed Steel Suburban 3-car DMU (51346, 51388, 59516) is stabled in the Up siding.

was running under diesel power, then that was only available if no traction power was required.

The Bluebell Railway has now chosen to embrace the place for preserved modern traction in Southern Railway history through its acquisition of Class 73/1 73133 *The Bluebell Railway* which has been accepted on a ten-year loan. Previously it has steadfastly refused to incorporate diesel or electric locomotives within its fleet, but now also embraces Class 33 33052 and a Class 09 shunter. These locomotives can prove useful in powering early morning low-demand services or when there is a fire-risk from the use of steam locomotives during prolonged spells of dry weather. The Class 73 can also prove useful for providing traction for engineering trains. 73107 is unique in having been modified for route learning purposes and was also the first of its class to be painted in civil engineers' 'Dutch' livery, although it also wore Network SouthEast and Mainline Freight blue.

Compared to the 1,420hp available from the Class 73 Electro-Diesels' traction motors type EE542 when drawing from third rail, the diesel performance available from the auxiliary English Electric 4SRKT Mk2 of 600hp was certainly more restrictive, though certainly adequate for, when required, it enabled the locomotives to work in yards not equipped with third rail and facilitated their use with engineering trains operating in locations where traction current through the third rail was switched off. It meant they were an ideal locomotive to use when involved with the Bournemouth electrification scheme (which meant that some of the Class 73s were moved away from their Class's home depot at Stewarts Lane).

Their versatility when working push-pull trains also proved especially useful on passenger workings between the Hampshire Coast and London Waterloo during the time when electric motors from Class 432/438 4-REPS were being refurbished for use in Wessex Electric class 442s ready for use in enhanced services provided to the newly electrified Bournemouth to Weymouth line. Five diagrams were provided using pairs of Class 73s initially, but eventually a single Class 73 was proven adequate from May 1987.

This train formation, as seen on page 80, makes quite an impression in its retro BR blue style livery whilst looking authentic when seen here attached to the Metropolitan red livery 4TC push-pull set, and recalls the use of the class 73 locomotives hauling similar 4TC sets used when they deputised for the 4-REPS as detailed above. The Class 73/2 proved sturdy and reliable locomotives hauling

DIESEL AND ELECTRIC LOCOMOTIVES • **79**

In the first picture, we see at Corfe Common, Swanage Railway, Sunday, 11 May 2008: Class 73/1 73107 *Spitfire*, operated by GBRF Eastleigh, at the rear of the 13.10 Swanage to Norden, formed of Class 423 EMU 4-Vep 3417 in BR blue, owned and restored by South West Trains for the latter days of slam-door workings. **In the second picture,** the same train formation is seen earlier passing Corfe Castle with 73107 *Spitfire* hauling the 12.30 Norden to Swanage, formed of Class 423 EMU 4-Vep 3417.

Harmans Cross, Swanage Railway, Saturday, 13 May 2023: GBRf Class 73/2 73201 *Broadlands* departs Harmans Cross with the 14.15 Swanage to Corfe Castle.

unpowered trailer ex-Mk.2F Class 488 coaching sets for the Gatwick Expresses until displaced by Class 460 units (derivative of the Alstom 'Juniper' EMUs with their distinctive streamlined front ends), able to keep to tight schedules while operating within the strictures of a busy suburban network on the Brighton main line. In some ways, this important duty remained an unsung virtue, taken for granted amidst a changing railway scene favouring units rather than traditional locomotives and coaches.

The versatility of the Class 73s saw them used on a wide variety of trains in the Southern Region area. Concerning non-passenger duties, they could be seen paired with Class 33s on parcels traffic, or single-handed hauling Travelling Post Office trains from Dover to and from Wembley Royal Mail hub and providing traction for hauling Civil Engineers' trains or heavy tanker trains. GB Railfreight now owns a fleet of these nearly sixty-year-old locomotives and operates the class in the South East on various excursion trains, work for Network Rail test-train duties, Civil Engineers' trains laden with ballast or sleepers, and also hauling Railhead Treatment Trains (RHTT) and Snow and Ice Treatment Trains to help with clearance during the winter with de-icing vehicles.

Corfe Common, Swanage Railway, Saturday, 13 May 2023: GBRf Class 73/1 73107 leads GBRf Class 73/2 73201 *Broadlands* with the Metropolitan red livery 4TC push-pull 4-carriage set forming the late-running 16.15 Swanage to Corfe Castle.

It is worth noting that there is an increasing practice on the European continent where a variety of container and freight operators are investing in Vectron electric locomotives equipped with last-mile diesel power modules (DPM) for use in serving destinations away from overhead electrified lines. In many ways, the Class 73 and 74 set the trend.

GBRf 73s tend to keep to their previous haunts on the Southern network, employed for duties such as working autumnal season RHTTs for Southeastern, while others have escaped to the wilds of Scotland. The Class 73/9s 73961-965, owned by GBRf, had their origins in a batch of Class 73/2s which were re-engineered by Brush Loughborough during 2014 to 2016. They were redesigned with modern electronic traction control systems and 1,600hp MTU R43L 4000 V8 engines. Their prime use is now with Network Rail. Duties with Caledonian Sleeper services have seen a further batch of GBRf operated Class 73/9 locomotives '73966 to 971' (from a mix of previous Class 73/0, 73/1 and 73/2) painted in Midnight Teal livery and used on these services to Fort William and Inverness. The third rail pick-up shoes have been retained but isolated. Pairs of these were intended to haul the Caledonian Sleeper trains from

82 • DIESEL AND ELECTRIC MOTIVE POWER ON THE SOUTHERN 1980s TO PRESENT

Honiton Bank, Saturday, 16 July 2016: in the first picture we see GBRf Class 73/9 73962 and 73963 heading to the west with an excursion from London Waterloo bound for Paignton and Torbay. In the second picture at the same location but looking west we see at the rear of this train GBRf Class 73/1 73107 which leads GBRf Class 73/1 73128 *O.V.S. Bulleid C.B.E.*

DIESEL AND ELECTRIC LOCOMOTIVES • 83

Edinburgh and Glasgow to their Highland destinations, replacing the Class 67s previously used. In practice, they proved inadequate for such and now provide electric train heating, while Class 66 locomotives provide the necessary tractive effort for the rugged terrain through which they operate.

Two new passing loops on the Salisbury to Exeter section of the London Waterloo to Exeter main line, that at Tisbury in 1986 and at Axminster in 2009, have permitted an hourly service along the route and additional trains between Yeovil Junction and Gillingham. This has seen enhanced use of the line between intermediate stations, especially east of Yeovil Junction. It is seen as desirable to extend the existing Tisbury loop eastwards to Dinton and westwards to a point beyond Tisbury station. At present, alternating trains stop either at Feniton or Whimple, which results in an irregular, less than hourly, service at these intermediate stations. An enhanced service would reduce overcrowding on the Exeter to Waterloo hourly services and facilitate an hourly path for diverted Exeter to Paddington services when engineering or flooding of the GWR main line (east of Exeter) dictates a requirement for such.

This train service actually went as far as Meldon Quarry during the time that the line was under ownership of the Dartmoor Railway Association. The swift reopening by GWR of the Okehampton branch in November 2021 exemplifies the case that 'where there's a will, there's a way'. Much evidence of the successful reopening of the Scottish Borders line in September 2015 showed that reopening of

Pinhoe, Saturday, 17 June 2023: GBRf Class 73/9 73962 leads 73964 with the 07.14 London Waterloo to Exeter St Davids excursion.

Okehampton, Dartmoor Railway, Sunday, 10 April 2005: Class 73/1 73134 in InterCity livery, on loan to the Dartmoor Railway at this time, is seen at the rear of the 13.35 ex-Sampford Courtenay, 14.00 Okehampton to Meldon. The stock includes two Mk. II First carriages, a Trailer Buffet and an ex-Parcels generator van.

extant routes where much of the original route had been protected from redevelopment was possible and remunerative. The Department for Transport (DfT) requested a proposal from GWR for the Okehampton line reopening, which GWR responded to in 2019 with an outline business case. The DfT 'Restoring your Railway' scheme injected momentum with close working between Network Rail, GWR and DfT to secure funding which was released in April 2021 and the railway opened to the public in November of the same year. The funding allowed Network Rail to purchase the route (Coleford Junction to Meldon Quarry) from Aggregate Industries, and to purchase Okehampton station from Devon County Council. Eleven miles of track was re-laid between Coleford Junction and Okehampton in just four weeks, which was record breaking (the earliest track on the route dated back to the 1930/40s, with some of the oldest components from 1908). This was followed by clearance, repair and renewal of drainage. Bridge and fencing repairs were completed and embankment stabilisation works undertaken. Significant clearance of several years' worth of vegetation was requisite along the route, and ecological licences acquired. The station building and canopy still remained in decent condition, and with restoration this further assisted the swift reinstatement of the passenger service.

EM/2 Class 77

Whilst this locomotive, which was built for the Manchester to Sheffield 'Woodhead' route supplied with overhead electrification which came into use by EM1 Class 76s from February 1952, may

DIESEL AND ELECTRIC LOCOMOTIVES • **85**

look out of place both in terms of location and electric power supply equipment, it may not be completely irrelevant. It was one of only seven Class EM/2 Class 77 locomotives which originally was intended to be a fleet of twenty-seven.

It can be argued that the electric power supply for the Southern Railway was exclusively via third rail, and for this the Southern Region Class CC (70) was built to accommodate some of the difficulties posed within the third rail system. Electric locomotives were encountering gaps in the third rail which were longer than the length of a locomotive, and these existed at numerous locations on the electrified network. Here power would be lost and a consequent jolt caused to the train which could result in buffer locking or even cause a train to stall if its speed was low and the momentum inadequate to carry it to the next section of third rail. In the Class CC locomotives, a 'booster' was provided which ensured adequate power was supplied via a flywheel-driven generator which provided power for enough momentum to enable the train to coast through gaps of around 100 feet if speed was at least 12mph. The Class CC was equipped both with pick-up shoes for power collection from the third rail and with a roof-mounted pantograph to collect current from overhead wires where such were supplied in railway yards which consequently had no third rail within parts of their confines.

London Waterloo, Saturday, 1 October 1988: Class EM/2 27000 *Electra* is seen on display; the locomotive had been repainted the previous summer into the former Brunswick green livery.

PART 2

Diesel Multiple Units and Railbus

Class 101

Weymouth, Sunday, 26 October 1986: Metro-Cammell Class 101 51509/59050/51513 is stabled, shortly after being transferred from Bristol to Cardiff 29 September 1986, in between duties from Bristol and Cardiff.

Understandably, in view of the comprehensive third rail providing the power source for EMUs across the Southern Region, the use of DMUs was restricted to routes lacking that infrastructure. Therefore, while many commuters across the U.K. in the 1970s and '80s enjoyed the generally solid ride provided by a variety of DMU types in contrast to third rail electric inner and outer suburban EMUs of the Southern (with the exceptions of Merseyside, the Wirral, Manchester to Bury and Tyneside where third rail systems existed), some Southern routes still required the provision of diesel traction. In the case of this photograph, the diesel train will diverge from the Southern after the short journey to Dorchester, and then make its way on traditional

Western Region rails to Castle Cary, Westbury, Bath, Bristol and possible onward to Cardiff.

This date was not the best for a Network SouthEast day to take place! In the previous week, six of the seven oaks at Sevenoaks had been felled by a severe storm, sections of Kent's network were blocked by literally rows of fallen trees and Reigate High Street carrying the A25 required careful navigation by motorists around a large fallen oak. This followed the now notorious advice from the Met Office that there wasn't any need to be concerned with warnings of an approaching hurricane! The picturesque North Downs line is non-electrified for two main sections totalling 29 miles. The longest stretch without electrification is 17 miles from Shalford to Reigate. Services of two trains per hour, one semi-fast and one stopper, using Class 166 DMUs are provided. Some sections allow speeds of up to 70mph, other sections are restricted to between 30 and 50mph. Capacity restraints at Guildford and from Redhill to Gatwick Airport limit opportunities for any enhanced service. It may be that trains equipped with batteries, similar to some of Merseyside's new Class 777, can provide an economically viable solution to the needs for the line's trains to be upgraded.

Reigate, Saturday, 24 October 1987 – a week after the Great Storm. Class 101 Metro-Cammell 53333/59105/51190 forms the 09.40 Reading to Reigate and Gatwick Airport. Here the third rail from Redhill electric terminates.

Class 118

The First Generation BRCW Class 118 diesel units were initially allocated to the Western Region, though latterly a few received Network SouthEast livery as during the late 1980s several of the Class were based at Reading and Old Oak Common.

The Dartmoor Line was the first line to be reopened under the government's 'Restoring Your Railway' programme with more than £40 million being invested. The agreed strategy has always been to retain the heritage feel of the station recalling that of the 1950s Southern Railway. Okehampton station has survived relatively intact during preservation under the banner of the Dartmoor Railway, with station buildings, footbridge, signal box and adjacent goods shed all remaining. The former ticket office received restoration as an authentic recreation of a 1950s ticket office, under a project carried out in collaboration with the Devon and Cornwall Rail Partnership. Integrated transport incorporates a bus link service via Lydford and Brentor to Tavistock, which thereby follows closely the Southern Railway route and nearly closes the gap via Bere Alston to Plymouth. Government funding is committed towards the reopening of the section of line from a location west of Tavistock to Plymouth, subject to an updated business case. This scheme will reinstate approximately five miles of track and deliver a new single

Okehampton, Saturday, 25 May 1985: Class 118 BRCW DMU 51309/59476/51324 forms a special 'Moors-Link' 10.38 service to Exeter. This was the first BR operated passenger train service on the branch since the line's closure to passengers in 1972.

platform station at Tavistock. The station would serve around 21,000 residents of Tavistock, Horrabridge, Lamerton, and Mary Tavy and will be operated as a Park and Ride facility with an anticipated hourly service.

Class 142 and 143 'Pacer' Railbus

Introduced from 1985-87, these were essentially buses on rails – their bodywork based on the Leyland National bus – in terms of their low cost, high density interior seating, lightweight diesel units (24-25 tonnes) powered by a Cummins LTA 10-Rf 225hp engine, and with hydraulic transmission. Commuters across northern and eastern England, and parts of the South West and Wales, had plenty of time to adjust to the roll and bounce of these trains, especially when they reached their maximum speed of 75mph. Indeed, they became notorious for their poor quality ride. There were concerns that these units did not always activate track circuits which saw their swift removal from Devon's lines to those where this did not seem such a problem. A further problem occurred with excessive flange squeal on tight curves caused by the long wheelbase and lack of bogies. This saw them removed from the Plymouth to Gunnislake and Cornish branch lines. With their relatively high entrance step, which deemed them unsuitable for disabled persons' access, from 1 January 2020 they could only operate when paired

Neopardy Road Bridge, near Yeoford, Saturday, 5 November 2011: First Great Western Class 142 'Pacer' 142009, with a First Great Western Class 153 at the rear, passes with the 13.43 Barnstaple to Exmouth.

with a Person of Reduced Mobility compliant class 150 or 153 (as seen here although on this occasion used for strengthening purposes).

The Class 143 diesel railcars were a slight improvement to the earlier Class 142 versions, and their bodies were built by Alexander, a bus company which had a good reputation for quality bus bodywork design. They were given a refurbish in later years and remained in service along the Barnstaple, Exmouth and Torbay branch lines much longer than intended owing to an ongoing shortage of more modern stock cascaded from other parts of the country (such as Thames Turbos from the North Downs line). The Barnstaple branch is essentially single line now, with several passing loops. This service will soon call at Crediton which has two platforms and historic station buildings which are well maintained, with the main station building housing a Community Interest Company operating out of the Station Tea Rooms.

New Bridge, Sunday, 2 October 2011: First Great Western Class 143 143611 approaches with the 13.55 Exeter Central to Barnstaple.

The twin red brick bridge seen in the picture below reflect the Devon Redlands soils. The underlying red sandstone and consequent red soil dominate the local landscape and are part of the red colour found in the traditional stone and cob farmsteads, hamlets and villages. The Down line on the left, with its platform remains, is the Okehampton branch, though disused here at the time of this picture, with any reopening of that branch just a distant hope. Little did anyone expect that the line would be transformed within eleven years when a timetabled service was re-introduced. During earlier years, the Barnstaple route was double track at this point and Yeoford a busy interchange station with extensive sidings and traffic in cattle, agriculture produce and equipment. Here some expresses from Waterloo were divided, with one portion bound for North Devon and the other for Tavistock and

DIESEL MULTIPLE UNITS AND RAILBUS • 91

Plymouth, or North Cornwall. Now just a request halt, it has the unusual claim to a free lending library of books kept in the waiting room so you can read whilst awaiting your train's arrival.

Overleaf is a busy scene which captures at least a little of this station and passing loop's heyday in the days of steam. After all, the prestigious 'Atlantic Coast Express' carrying passengers for Barnstaple and Ilfracombe hauled by a West Country Pacific would have passed through here; likewise Warship Class 42s hauling Ilfracombe to Exeter St Davids services in the late 1960s. The Up platform station buildings were built by the North Devon Railway in 1854 and later transferred to the LSWR. Impressive is the gable-ended double-fronted asymmetrical building of Restrained Tudor Gothic style in the centre of which was the ticket office. The house and ticket office consist of two storeys, the luggage store and waiting room at the north west end are single storey. The station serves the villages of Chawleigh and Chulmleigh, with passengers reliant on cars to reach their trains.

Yeoford, Saturday,
5 November 2011: A pair of First Great Western Class 143 'Pacers', with 143620 at the rear, departs with the 10.53 Exmouth/11.27 Exeter St Davids to Barnstaple.

Eggesford, Saturday, 28 January 2012: on the left, we see Class 143 143603 operating the 12.27 Exeter St Davids to Barnstaple; on the right, Class 143 143611 leads Class 143 143621 operating the 12.43 Barnstaple to Exmouth.

Many of the Class 142, 143 and 144 railbuses have found homes on the UK's widespread preservation railways, some of which have more than one example. Acquired at low purchase cost, they fill a niche where off-peak services can be much more economically provided than the alternative steam locomotives burning expensive coal or heavy diesels consuming fuel. Some lines have refused to compromise their fleets, considering them to be inappropriate for the heritage atmosphere that they seek to recreate.

The Exeter to Barnstaple line remains a wonderful branch line to reminisce about the traditional railway away from the main line. There are station houses extant and carefully maintained by their owners at most of the stations between Newton St Cyres and Chapelton, along with tended gardens on the platforms which bring a splash of colour from spring to autumn. The character of this Southern branch line in Devon is retained by the various crossing keepers' cottages, concrete permanent way huts, and the many viaducts crossing the Rivers Taw and Yeo. Class 158/9 and Class 166 trains now offer a much smoother ride, past the red brick farms and thatched cottages and barns,

Lapford, Sunday, 13 May 2012: First Great Western Class 143 'Pacer' 143621 at the rear of a Class 150 departs with the 12.03 Exeter St Davids to Barnstaple.

many of the latter constructed with their characteristic Devon cob walls – a mixture of local red earth, water, manure and straw applied in horizontal layers

Class 150 'Sprinter' and Class 153 'Super Sprinter'

The Second Generation 'Sprinter' units at least provided a more stable ride and higher level of interior comfort than the 'Pacers', although they were built for suburban commuter use rather than lengthy rural lines with potential journeys of an hour or more. Their regular use on Penzance to Exeter services, for example, must have set endurance records for those unfortunate enough to travel the full distance. Introduced to replace the ageing 'heritage' DMUs, they began to appear in increasing numbers across the north west, West Yorkshire and the Midlands during the mid-1980s and would have been seen on the Southern at Salisbury with trains from Bristol to Portsmouth and at Exeter Central on services to Exmouth, Torbay and Barnstaple.

The station at Newton St. Cyres a request halt, features much of the character mentioned above concerning the traditional Southern branch line in Devon, including the floral displays. The rear decking of the adjacent pub overlooks passing trains, verdant foliage permitting!

Newton St Cyres, Sunday, 2 October 2011: First Great Western Class 150/2 150265 forms the 11.26 Barnstaple to Exeter Central.

An interesting point is that the prototype Class 150 was used on the Reading to Basingstoke service. Their variety of operators ensured a colourful selection of liveries which, when occasions involved units being transferred from one region or operator to another, resulted in the livery or branding consequently changing, although not always immediately. It was hence possible to see a 'Heart of Wessex' branded Class 150 in the depths of Cornwall. Their presence on Bristol to Portsmouth services meant that they traversed Southern metals at Salisbury and thence onwards to Portsmouth.

There is clear evidence at Yeoford of the erstwhile Down line platform whose booking office even as late as 1928 was still issuing close to 13,000 tickets a year. That's evidence of a local mainly agrarian community making use of their local railway station – but of course that was at a time when only wealthy people owned cars, and when a bus provided a much slower, meandering journey than the train which at Exeter Central provided convenient access to Exeter's shopping facilities. In earlier times, Yeoford station even featured, across from the existing Up platform, a refreshments room on this central island platform, no doubt catering to the needs of passengers transferring between the North Devon line to Bideford

DIESEL MULTIPLE UNITS AND RAILBUS • 95

Gunstone Mill Bridge, Saturday, 5 November 2011: Front: First Great Western Class 153 153377 with, at rear, First Great Western Class 150/2 150248, passes with the 11.43 Barnstaple to Exmouth.

Yeoford, Saturday, 25 November 2023: Class 150/2 150249 passes through with the 12.33 Exeter Central to Okehampton.

and the Okehampton line which also served north Cornwall as far as Wadebridge and Padstow. The final 'Atlantic Coast Express' train departed Padstow hauled by West Country Class 21C123 *'Blackmoor Vale'* (renumbered 34023 by BR) on 5 September 1964.

Given that this train, seen at Bere Alston, will take just under 30 minutes to reach Plymouth station from here, a car journey also from here to Plymouth station may take the same time during the day, with little to choose from, but at rush hour it can take at least twice as long with extensive queues and slow moving traffic for at least six miles. The line to and from Gunnislake, from where the train has come, is slow with many sharp curves and several steep gradients imposing severe speed restrictions, with that from Calstock – seen here – clambering upwards from 1 in 264 to 1 in 37 towards Bere Alston station. Such was enough to see off the Pacer railcars from their use on the branch – and others in Cornwall – because they could not cope with the severity of these curves and grades, suffering severe wheel flats from excessive flange squeal while screeching around the twisting curves.

On the following page we have the opportunity to compare the transition in liveries applied by First Great Western during the relevant era and also to consider the depth and width of this graceful 120 foot high viaduct which crosses the River Tamar as well as the border between Devon and Cornwall. Readers who are familiar with this location will appreciate why this remarkable

Bere Alston,
Monday,
7 November 2016:
First Great Western
Class 150 150266
arrives with the
13.45 Gunnislake to
Plymouth.

landmark is a favoured photographic location in all seasons. Most impressive are its twelve 60 ft. wide arches along its 850 ft. length. At high tide, the minimum clearance for shipping is 110 ft. Its construction was completed in 1908, and opened on 2nd March as part of the Plymouth, Devonport and South Western Junction Railway. The line through to Callington was absorbed into the LSWR in 1923 when incorporated into the Southern Railway. During the early 1960s freight traffic declined along the branch and DMUs replaced steam locomotive-hauled trains. Poor road access to the area served enabled the viaduct to remain open for passenger traffic, as it continued to provide a key link across the

Right and below: **First picture:** Calstock Viaduct, Monday, 7 November 2016: First Great Western Class 150/2 150266 crosses with the 11.45 Gunnislake to Plymouth. Second picture: Calstock Viaduct, Tuesday, 29 November 2016: An unidentified First Great Western Class 150/2 crosses with the 11.45 Gunnislake to Plymouth.

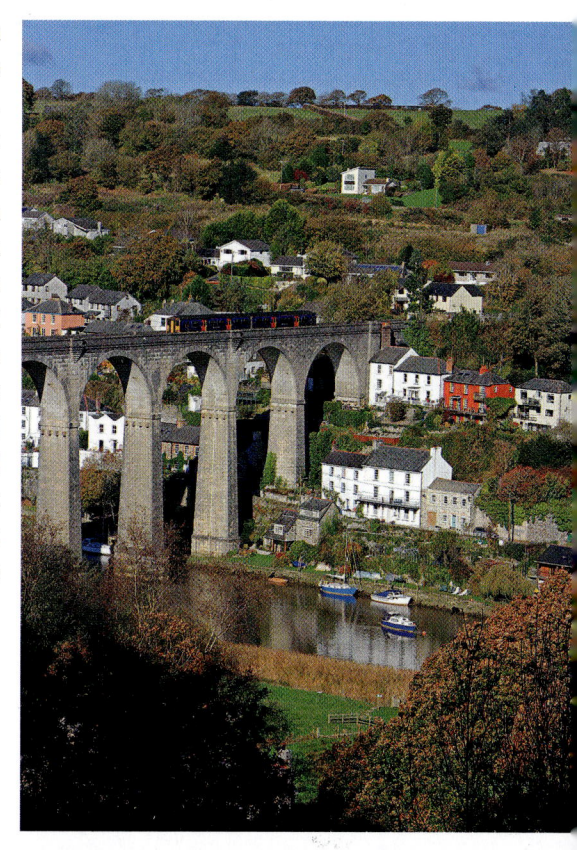

Tamar. However, the section from Gunnislake to Callington was closed 5 November 1966 and all freight services withdrawn from that date.

Here is another station on the Tamar Valley line which is relatively remote for those travelling the 23 miles by road to Plymouth city centre as opposed to the 8 miles by rail. It is situated on the peninsula between the Rivers Tamar and Tavy.

With its Southern platform canopy, station building and signal box, each in appropriate Southern green, and accompanied by some sentry-like semaphore signals, a remarkable reminiscence of the station's LSWR origins cannot be avoided. The fact that the station building and signal box (the latter previously in use at Pinhoe) are both privately owned by a dedicated rail enthusiast certainly helps. The goods yard at the south end of the station, closed in 1965, is used for privately owned storage of some carriages and other rolling stock including a former LMS twelve-wheeled 1950s sleeping carriage. The 'Tamar Belle' enterprise offered by the Tamar Belle Heritage Group Visitor Centre enables visitors to see the collection of railway-linked features such as a turntable and yard crane. Class 108 Derby Lightweight and Class 101 Metro-Cammell DMUs were used on this scenic line from the early 1990s after the

Bere Ferrers, Friday, 11 March 2016: First Great Western Class 150/2 150249 arrives with the 13.45 Gunnislake to Plymouth.

Class 142 Pacers were removed from service on this line for reasons discussed above, and Class 150 and Class 153 units were introduced to the line from 1992 thereafter.

On a day which saw local roads covered in ice with a consequent risk of accidents, the railway continued to serve the Tamar Valley with its usual efficiency. The ex-LSWR Signal Box was opened 12 May 1890 to serve the goods yard; Bere Alston station was opened for passenger traffic on 2 June 1890 as part of the new Plymouth, Devonport & South Western Junction Railway line from Lydford to Devonport. The Box was closed 7 September 1970 and replaced by a ground frame for use in reversing the Plymouth to Gunnislake branch trains. On 6 May 1968, the ex-LSWR main line beyond the east end of Bere Alston station was closed completely. This radical reduction in the railway service in West Devon left Bere Alston as the terminus of a double-track branch from Plymouth, served only by local trains. After the disappearance of freight traffic, all the remaining sidings at Bere Alston were removed. The branch was re-aligned to make a new junction at the south end of the former Down platform and the junction is now controlled by a 2-lever ground frame, released by a key on the single-line train staff. Trains for Gunnislake now arrive at the former Down platform and

Bere Alston, Sunday, 20 December 2009: First Great Western Class 153 153318 at the platform with the 11.40 Plymouth to Gunnislake.

Gunstone Mill Bridge, Saturday, 5 November 2011: First Great Western Class 153 153373 leads a First Great Western Class 142 forming the 11.53 Exmouth to Barnstaple.

then reverse on to the branch. The island platform is out of use and the footbridge demolished.

Knowledgeable passengers and rail enthusiasts will know that the Class 153 will provide the superior ride as compared to the Railbus. The high capacity of the Super Sprinter is partly disguised by its length, being a much longer vehicle as can be seen when comparing the two coupled up as viewed here. The single-car Class 153 units were built by British Leyland as 2-car Class 155s and then converted by Hunslet-Barclay at Kilmarnock in 1991-92 where a second driving cab was fitted to each vehicle of the Class 155s. In recent years ScotRail has introduced Class 153s modified to carry extra bicycles and luggage onto West Highland line services between Glasgow and Oban, working with Class 156s at the time of writing. They are marketed as ScotRail Highland Explorer and 153373 now provides such a modified purpose. April 2023 saw its first such use when, paired with 156500, it worked the 18:23 service from Glasgow Queen Street.

Class 158 and 159 Express Sprinters

Interestingly, 4-TC sets hauled by Class 33s previously saw use on some of the diagrams between Portsmouth and Cardiff. The through route was once the territory of Class D15 4-4-0 steam locomotives. The viaduct spans the River Wallington, a northern arm of Portsmouth Harbour. Built in 1848, 735 yards length, it is constructed with seventeen round-headed arches in brick and a yellow brick string course.

The Class 158 Express Sprinters were designed to replace locomotive hauled trains on many longer distance domestic services under the Provincial banner. The intention was to provide a high standard of comfort and performance with low running costs in order to ensure a reliable and financially viable fleet of trains across the Regions. October 1989 saw the first unit, 158701, emerge from Derby Litchurch Lane, with numbering from 158701–158872 allocated to standard units and 158901–158910 allocated to sets owned and operated by West Yorkshire PTE. There were three varieties of power unit, with Cummins 350hp engines supplied to the standard 2- and 3-car units, Perkins type-2006 350hp engines supplied to a batch of non-standard units and higher output 400hp Cummins supplied to the Class 158863-872 and Class 159s. The set seen in the photograph was one of the sets based at Cardiff. On Southern metals they would have been seen between Salisbury, Southampton and Portsmouth or Brighton.

Fareham Wallington Viaduct, Sunday, 11 October 1998: A Class 158 crosses with the 09.30 Cardiff Central to Portsmouth Harbour.

Autumn 2020 saw the Class 158s settle into diagrams from Exeter to Barnstaple. Such followed their belated introduction to the Barnstaple branch, caused by the delay in Thames Chiltern releasing their Turbo units to Bristol. These trains, either formed of two or three cars with an additional single Class 158 Driving Motor Coach, provide a substantial improvement both in quality of ride and interior comfort as compared to the Class 150s and Class 143s which had previously ploughed their way through the rural idyll landscape of mid-Devon. Such was the transition that it was now possible to pour a cup of tea from a thermos and catch it *all* in the cup whilst travelling at speed around the many curves that characterise this Southern time capsule.

The quality of ride and comfortable seating provided by Class 159s ensures an enjoyable journey along the Southern for those passengers travelling to the South West by the ex-Southern route to Exeter. They were ordered as a follow-on order to the Class 158s and the Network SouthEast Director Chris Green's decision to require an uprated power unit to be incorporated in the 3-car Class 159 for the demanding territory of the line has certainly paid off. Usually, three units work as far as Salisbury and two continue to Exeter although for off-peak times, some diagrams see only one unit to serve the section to and from Exeter which does tend to create overcrowding from Exeter Central on London-bound services.

Newton St Cyres, Saturday, 26 March 2022: Class 158 158958 passes through with the 14.35 Barnstaple to Exeter Central.

DIESEL MULTIPLE UNITS AND RAILBUS • 103

Clapham Junction, Wednesday, 5 July 2023: South Western Railway Class 159 159004 departs with the 15.20 London Waterloo to Exeter St Davids.

Quite certainly the regular stop/start pattern at the many stations and heavy gradients which characterised the route took their toll on the Class 50s and Class 47/7s as detailed above. On the single line to the west beyond Salisbury, where prompt time keeping was requisite to avoid delaying waiting trains at the few loops while heading in the opposite direction, the need to find a replacement fleet of trains became imperative. Network SouthEast welcomed

Tisbury, Sunday, 12 April 2015: South West Trains Class 159 159021 departs with the 10.25 Exeter St Davids to London Waterloo.

with relish the first Class 159 delivered in January 1993. To accompany this, a new traction maintenance depot, situated on the north side of Salisbury station, opened in 1992 to service the new fleet of trains. This greatly facilitated restoration of reliability and punctuality of services along the route. The investment of £3 million to enable the provision of a fully modernised fleet-dedicated depot at Salisbury in October 2009, at which further specialist attention to maintenance and stocks of parts would help address the needs of care for the fleet of Class 159 trains using the line, reinforced the priority henceforth being given to operations along the line. The completion of a new fuelling shed helped to increase fuelling capacity at the depot.

The reason behind the Salisbury to Exeter route being reduced to single line in 1967 was that rationalisation led to the concentration of traffic on selected routes to avoid that which was considered at the time to be duplication. The GWR line from Paddington to the West Country via Newbury and Somerton became the principal route while the Southern Region line from Waterloo was reduced to secondary status. The reduction to single line started with the section from Wilton South to Templecombe and finished with that from Chard Junction to Pinhoe. The existing double track from Salisbury was retained as far

Axminster, Thursday, 17 August 2023: South Western Railway Class 159 159107 departs with the 11.25 Exeter St Davids to London Waterloo.

as the former station at Wilton South from where the line was thence singled as far as Templecombe, with an intermediate passing loop at Gillingham, and from Templecombe double track was retained as far as Sherborne. Beyond there, the line became single as far as Pinhoe, with the exception of passing loops at Chard Junction and Honiton. This left four closed stations where trains could conceivably have to wait, whereas only three open stations – Honiton, Sherborne and Gillingham – had double track in situ.

Consequent to the institution of the single line arrangements referred to above, understandably the original plan proved unworkable with a need for improved flexibility to enable the passing of late running trains, and the section of line between Yeovil Junction and Sherborne was reinstated in 1967, as it had yet to be lifted. A loop was much later reinstated at Tisbury in 1986, thus splitting the very long section from Gillingham to Wilton, although it had to be located outside the station because the Down side platform had been sold off. Axminster station was provided with a second platform and passing loop in 2009, and this has further assisted punctuality along the line, although late running of Down London trains does still occasionally delay Up trains at Pinhoe for over ten minutes, as I have experienced!

Honiton, Wednesday, 14 June 2023: South Western Railway Class 159 159018 forms the rear 3-car set with 159009 leading the departing 18.26 Exeter St Davids to London Waterloo.

It is worth noting that the bus links from the stations at Axminster to Lyme Regis and from Honiton to Sidmouth enable rail travellers to access these Dorset and South Devon coastal towns previously served by Southern Railway branches and in some way therefore sustain that historic link with the LSWR. It seems likely that a fleet of dual-mode units capable of drawing from third rail electric and from onboard battery power may replace the Class 159s.

Class 165 Network Turbo and Class 166 Network Express Turbo

These DMUs have become displaced from their traditional haunts along the GWR main line from London Paddington where, as part of the Thames Trains franchise, they reached as far as Newbury and Bedwyn, Oxford and Basingstoke alongside the branches to Windsor & Eton, Henley and Marlow. These 2- and 3-car units have been reliable and efficient in providing commuters travelling to and from these destinations with adequate if rather cramped seating. The reason for their displacement is the completion of electrification along the route from London to Reading and Didcot

Bincombe Tunnel (south portal), Saturday, 6 August 2022: GWR Class 165 165130 forms the rear set of two as it approaches the tunnel mouth with the 12.15 Weymouth to Westbury.

DIESEL MULTIPLE UNITS AND RAILBUS • 107

and their replacement by Class 387 and Crossrail/Elizabeth Line Class 345 electric units.

With Weymouth's beach packed with day trippers enjoying some relatively rare hot sunshine, there is likely to be a limited number of passengers wishing to travel away from the popular resort during the middle of the afternoon, although those who are on board will be enjoying the extra leg room that these 3-car units provide, appropriate for the longer distances for which these units were designed, and the air-conditioning will also no doubt be much appreciated. Their spacious interior and smooth running at speeds faster than provided for with the Chiltern Railways Class 165s is impressive. Based in Bristol St Philip's Marsh depot, these units now spend their time on services into Wales as well as into Dorset, Somerset and Devon.

Demonstrating their recent introduction to services from Exeter to Barnstaple, the autumnal red and gold hues accommodate this Class 166 particularly well. Class 158/9s offer the alternative on the route – and in my opinion provide an even better level of comfort given their refurbishment. The Okehampton branch platform seen on the left is not considered economically viable and such maybe

Upwey Bank, Saturday, 6 August 2022: GWR Class 166 166205 ascends the demanding gradient with the 16.15 Weymouth to Great Malvern.

Yeoford, Saturday, 25 November 2023: GWR Class 166 166215 departs with the 12.19 Exeter St Davids to Barnstaple service.

justified, for the local community are reliant on their own vehicles for traversing the rural lanes to villages far away from the railway and are unlikely to be tempted to use the train unless they have no alternative. It is interesting that so little has changed at this location since that seen in the photograph of the Class 143 taken in autumn 2011 (as seen on page 91).

PART 3

Diesel Electric Multiple Units

Class 201-203 'Hastings' DEMU 6-car units

The concept of mounting the engine within the coach body of a diesel unit would have been familiar to those who had travelled in France in the 1950s and seen the SNCF Class X 3800 diesel railcar 'Picasso' units which were most distinctive with the driver's cab mounted off-centre above the unit body which contained at one end the engines. In Britain, it addressed the need to fit the English Electric 4SRKT 500hp engines into the special narrow body design of the diesel-electric units that would work the Tonbridge to Hastings route. The contractors for the 32 mile Tonbridge to Hastings line, Fox, Henderson & Co., experienced significant financial difficulties and had tried to reduce their losses by installing only four courses of bricks in the eight tunnels along the line. This was instead of the six courses for which they were contracted and the consequence was that the Mountfield Tunnel near Robertsbridge collapsed. It would have been an enormous expense to rebuild one of the most extensive tunnel systems in England, and the South Eastern Railway solved the problem by installing two additional courses of bricks in each of the tunnels. This inevitably reduced the loading gauge of the line, and it was thereafter necessary to build especially narrow rolling stock to operate the line.

Tonbridge, Thursday, 16 August 1984: Class 201 'Hastings' DEMU 1014 powers away at the rear of a Down service to Hastings.

110 • DIESEL AND ELECTRIC MOTIVE POWER ON THE SOUTHERN 1980s TO PRESENT

Consequent to the problems referred to above, it was decided that the Tonbridge to Hastings line would not be electrified as there would be problems fitting in the third rail. A design for narrower-bodied DEMUs to work the line was proceeded with. The carriages were similar in design to those of the EMUs operating Southern lines, and the onboard diesel engine would power the standard electric traction motors. Twenty-three narrow bodied 6-car sets formed of a driving motor coach at each end and four trailers were supplied during 1957, built at Eastleigh works. Along with other diesel EMUs these were nicknamed 'Thumpers' by the rail enthusiast fraternity because of the sound emitted by their

Rye Station and Signal Box, Friday, 27 July 2001: two views of preserved Class 201 Hastings line DEMU Unit 1001, with driving motor cars carrying names 60000 *Hastings* and 60018 *Tunbridge Wells* in BR Green livery, preserved at St Leonards Railway Engineering and on hire to Connex South Central owing to a shortage of Class 207 DEMUs, here operating the 11.31 Hastings to Ashford 'Marshlink' service (a brand which also included services from Ashford and Hastings to Eastbourne).

English Electric traction motors which literally sounded as if they were thumping at something. Initially, pairs of these sets worked through to London Charing Cross or Cannon Street.

The Class 203 'Hastings' DEMUs differed from the Class 201 and 202 units in that they carried a trailer with buffet facilities and were delivered new in 1958. Based at a new purpose-built depot at St Leonards, near Hastings, the anticipated ten-year lifespan of the 'Hastings' units was expected to keep the Tonbridge to Hastings service running until an alternative and preferred long-term option to electrify the route could be fulfilled. From 1972–77, British Railways also used them further afield for operating regular Saturdays-only Brighton to Exeter diagrams, formed of a pair of sets including a buffet. Popular demand saw them work several rail tours in the 1980s visiting such locations on Southern territory as Weymouth Quay and Laira Bridge across the Plym estuary. Corrosion of their bodywork, no doubt assisted by the salty sea air at St Leonards, and eventual electrification of the line in 1983, which also involved single-tracking of the line through its troublesome tunnels, saw them withdrawn after the Spring of 1986 and replaced by EMUs. In the care of the Hastings Diesel Group, they have found preservation in the form of a 4-car Class 201/202

Portsmouth and Southsea, 11 April 1987: right: Class 207 DEMU 207009, left: ex-Hastings class 203 DEMU unit Driving Motor Saloon BSO 60045, part of 6-car set 1037, on the 11.22 Southampton to Portsmouth Harbour.

set including 60000 and 60018 (previously part of set 1013) as featured in the previous two photographs. In addition to regularly working over four years the Connex South Central 'Marshlink' services illustrated, they also fulfilled a fourteen-month hire to Anglia Railways for use on local services between Norwich and Yarmouth/Lowestoft which ran from July 1998 to September 1999.

Class 205

Worthy of note here are the London, Brighton & South Coast Railway (LB&SCR) platform canopy supports and foreground line which is part of the former Tunbridge Wells branch, mothballed and now preserved by the Spa Valley Railway which owns the station buildings to the right. This station now constitutes separate parts, with the section seen on the left served by National Rail Southern Trains, which in past times followed a route to Croydon, that on the right serving the preserved line to Tunbridge Wells West. The Wealden Line served by Southern Trains continues south to Uckfield where the original station was replaced in 1991 by a single platform situated on the previous London-bound line north of the B1202, which removed the need for the level crossing there. This line once connected Lewes to Tunbridge Wells and takes its nomination from the chalk hills of the North and South Downs known as 'The Weald'. Withdrawal of services south of Uckfield

Eridge, Monday, 31 July 2000: Class 205 DEMU 205001 in Connex livery with the 11.00 Uckfield, 11.18 Eridge to Oxted.

in May 1969 was partly due to the state of Lewes Viaduct which had deteriorated considerably, its renovation and restoration not justified by British Railways. Services to Tunbridge Wells West continued until July 1985.

The classification of the Southern's diesel-electric multiple units (DEMUs) was based on the number of coaches comprising the unit and also the area in which they would operate. Therefore the 2-car units built to serve the non-electrified lines in Hampshire became '2H.' Initially a total of eighteen 2H DEMUs were built at Eastleigh. Their design was based on the Mk 1 coach and shared exterior and interior features. The power was provided by one English Electric 4SRKT 500hp engine mounted within the Driving Motor Brake Second Open carriage. The two carriages forming these sets soon proved inadequate to cater for the passenger demand and intermediate trailers were inserted into them, with their consequent reclassification to '3H.' A second batch of these units was provided for the Hastings to Ashford 'Marshlink'. Closure or electrification of various branches on which they operated saw the units, later redesignated as Class 205, serving a wider area including the Uckfield to London services which were also operated by sister Class 207 DEMUs.

Although in the early 1960s the Western Region had supplied DMUs for the Reading to Basingstoke services, with some continuing to Southampton and Portsmouth, the Southern required additional

Oxted, Saturday, 18 June 1994: Class 205 3-car DEMUs, left: 205018 shunts e.c.s. into the side bay after arriving with the 16.00 from Uckfield; right background: Class 205 stabled.

Micheldever, Tuesday, 9 August 1988: Class 205 3-car DEMU 205031 calls with the 13.55 Reading to Portsmouth Harbour.

units to replace these for the hourly Reading to Southampton Terminus service from June 1962. The Class 205s therefore helped meet such a requirement. The use of '3H' sets on the Alton to Winchester route was less successful owing to the steep gradients which impacted on their timekeeping, and the sets on this line were reduced to 2-car formations to compensate for such. That line now sees a preserved Class 205 set providing occasional services, and another line now in preservation that once saw these DMUs replace steam is the Swanage Railway, where they could be seen providing services to Worgret Junction and Wareham.

A green 2-car Hampshire DEMU operating in Hampshire! Such is preservation's ability to recreate genuine train types passing through typical landscapes through which they could have been seen providing services when in their heyday. Mind you, not all was as glossy as suggested here. When the Bristol to Portsmouth locomotive hauled coaching stock was replaced in the 1970s by these units, there were many complaints about the consequent overcrowding and lack of WCs in two of the 3-car sets. My own recollection of travelling in these units from Southampton to Portsmouth Harbour was that they provided a lively ride especially when sitting near the engine compartment, and enjoying the classic

Above and left:
First picture: Near Medstead & Four Marks; second picture: North Street near Ropley, 'Watercress Line,' Sunday, 9 July 2017: Class 205 2-car DEMU 1125 passes with afternoon services to and from Alresford to Alton.

thumping noise emanating from their working hard away from stations and up and down the gradients such as the 1 in 70 west of Fareham. Their use on the Salisbury to Reading via Basingstoke trains would have certainly given them a chance to stretch their legs.

The route to Eridge was closed 6 July 1985. Tunbridge Wells West Stabling Point was closed a little later on 10 August, facilitating empty coaching stock moves away from the depot with the resident Classes 205 and 207 DEMUs transferred to Selhurst and New Cross Gate. The connection with the Hastings line at Grove Junction was removed the day after closure and the spur between Tunbridge Wells West and Grove Junction was lifted shortly afterwards. Somewhat bizarrely, the site was not restricted to access during my rather cold February visit of 1986 and it was possible to walk along the platforms and cross the various lines left literally in situ. The once 5-platform grandiose station, opened in 1866 simply named Tunbridge Wells, appeared as if – literally and metaphorically – frozen in time. There were no longer any rail vehicles, although one wonders if the infrastructure had been left in place because units had previously remained stabled there for a short time after closure

First picture: Tunbridge Wells West DEMU Depot and stabling point, Saturday, 28 April 1984: Class 205 and Class 207 'Oxted' DEMU sets stabled. Second picture: Tunbridge Wells West Station, DEMU Depot and stabling point, Saturday, 22 February 1986. View to the east through the lines leading to the now- disused DEMU stabling point.

of the depot and stabling point. Some reports refer to the rails and associated buildings being in situ a full three years after closure. On the north side of the station there was a 4-road engine shed which later passed into the ownership of the Spa Valley Railway which now runs from a single platform at the site. The derelict goods yard became home to a Sainsbury's supermarket.

It was August 1997 that saw the fledgling 3½ mile long line from Tunbridge Wells West to Groombridge reopened in preservation, after BR had closed it in 1985. It was extended to Birchden Junction in 2004 and to Eridge, at 5½ miles length, in March 2011. Originating in the East Grinstead, Groombridge & Tunbridge Wells Railway and finished by the LB&SCR, this cross-country line from Three Bridges to East Grinstead was opened in 1855 and extended to Groombridge and Tunbridge Wells by 1866, while the line from Brighton to Groombridge via Eridge opened in 1868. Tunbridge Wells West shed was established in 1891 to service the steam locomotive fleet operating the line. The DEMUs operated the route from the 1960s transition from steam to diesel, until the closure to traffic. The Tunbridge Wells & Eridge Railway Preservation Society adopted a remit to save the line. Although Sainsbury's had purchased the station site at Tunbridge Wells West for their new superstore, the former engine shed fortunately survived, even if deprived of track and roof, and the station building was redeveloped in to a restaurant.

Groombridge, Sunday, 25 October 2015: Class 205 2-car DEMU 1133 forms the rear set as it departs with the midday Tunbridge Wells West to Eridge. It is visiting from the Lavender Line.

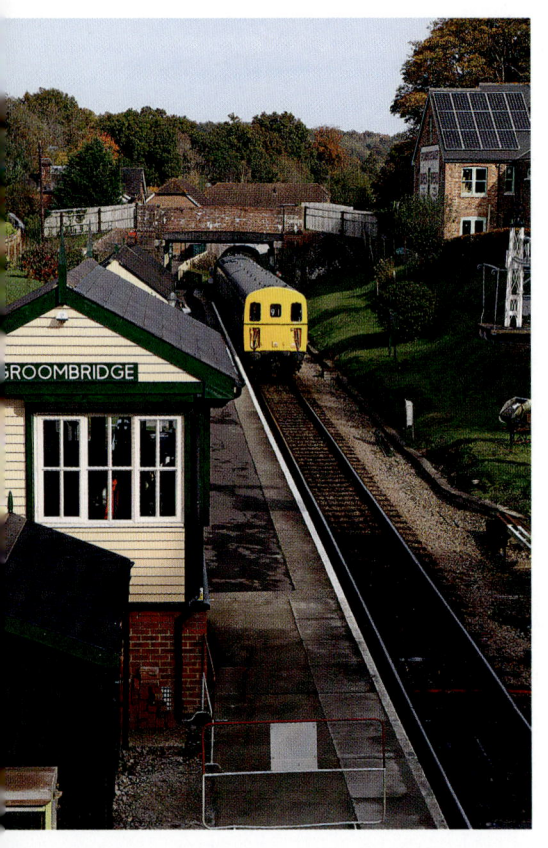

Sainsbury's generously sponsored major repairs to the locomotive shed and thus enabled it to become the headquarters of the railway.

Class 207

During the mid-1990s, the preservation line was renamed the 'Spa Valley Railway' which combined reference to the railway's operating from the Spa town of Royal Tunbridge Wells and its passing through the Valley of the High Weald to Eridge. Determined to reach Eridge, complex negotiations with Network Rail finally resulted in the line achieving its goal in 2011 of running into the station at Eridge which remains its southern terminus. Thus DEMU 1317 is a genuine part of the line's past and present, having operated the route in BR service until the last day prior to its closure, when it

Left and below: **Groombridge, Sunday,** 25 October 2015: Class 207 'Oxted' 2-car DEMU 1317 (207017) forms the front 'thumper' set as it arrives with an early afternoon service from Tunbridge Wells West to Eridge.

also formed the final Eridge to Tunbridge Wells West service, and now to be found providing services for the Spa Valley Railway. The third carriage of this unit, at the time of the photograph under restoration, completes the set's original 3-car formation of DMBSO S60142, TC S60616, DTSO S60916.

The station at Groombridge is situated adjacent to the original LB&SCR station which passengers starting their journey here walk past and is visible in this photograph beyond the overbridge. The Southern Region DEMU headcode 91 suggests a diagram from Charing Cross to Canterbury West or Margate via Orpington.

Remarkable is the fact that my accurate camera clock records the time of the train's arrival at Groombridge to be 13.17!

The BR blue and white livery when kept clean was smart and reminds us of the 1980s era prior to privatisation's multicoloured variety. The signal box was built entirely by volunteers and houses the old lever frame from the Birchden Junction signal box, where the lines from Oxted and Tunbridge converge. This became operational in August 2014 and now controls movements through the station when two or more trains are running, as here, or when services terminate at Groombridge. A clear view is afforded here of the original station seen beyond the overbridge. The nineteen Class 207 3-car DEMUs were part of an order for use on the Oxted line and were delivered in 1962. They were originally formed of a DMBS, a

Groombridge, Sunday,
25 October 2015: Class 207 'Oxted' 2-car DEMU 1317 (207017) forms the rear set as it departs with an early afternoon service from Tunbridge Wells West to Eridge.

Eastbourne, Saturday, 7 September 1996: Class 207/1 DEMU 207201 is seen having arrived with the 14.54 from Ashford. A second unit can be seen in the distance by the signal box. They still carry their Network SouthEast livery.

Trailer Composite Lavatory (TCL) and a Driving Trailer Second Saloon. Their cabs were built with steel reinforced fibreglass which was similar to the CIGs. Owing to the restricted clearance in the Somerhill Tunnel, on the section of line from Tonbridge to Tunbridge Wells West, their bodywork was built to 8ft 6 ins width. They were concentrated on the trunk routes from London Victoria and London Bridge to East Grinstead, Oxted and Tunbridge Wells and from London to Brighton via Uckfield.

The Class 207s saw several revisions to their formations to facilitate their capacity for an increasing number of passengers. The unit seen here was one of those into which was inserted a refurbished Class 411 4-CEP trailer second which became available in 1996 after that Class of EMU was withdrawn and reformed into 3-car sets. As a result, their appearance was somewhat imbalanced owing to the different designs of bodywork in these revised formations.

Although they spent their lives almost without exception on the dedicated routes referred to above, their area of operation later widened to take in the Ashford to Hastings 'Marshlink' route along which this unit is operating. It passes through some very attractive countryside including Romney Marsh and the historic fourteenth century Cinque Ports of Winchelsea and Rye.

By the early 1990s, the unreformed Class 207 units were sometimes found working on the Western section of the Southern, and could be seen – as here – operating Portsmouth to Southampton and Salisbury to Reading services. My fleet list book for 1997 shows it was still based at St Leonards depot (rather than at Eastleigh where some of the Class 205s would have been based, although 205017 was at this time also based at St Leonards).

A 2-car Class 207 set, 1305, has taken up residence on the previously strictly steam-only Bluebell Railway which has observed an exclusive steam presence in its heritage operations. This has been enabled by the Coulsdon Old Vehicle and Engineering Society

DIESEL ELECTRIC MULTIPLE UNITS • 121

Hastings, Monday, 3 August 1998: Class 207/1 DEMU 207201, including the centre car Trailer Second which is from Class 411 4-CEP 1546, departs with the 11.34 Hastings to Ashford; the signal box and semaphores retain a traditional railway landscape still escaping the lack of character which often results from modernisation.

St Denys, Saturday, 11 April 1987: Class 207 East Sussex DEMU 207003 and Class 205 Hampshire DEMU 205017 form the 10.33 Portsmouth Harbour to Salisbury service.

who have kindly donated the unit for this purpose. It will facilitate the railway's storyboard of the immediate post-steam era of the Southern Railway, and accompany the line's Class 09 and Class 33 in portraying that specific period of time. This unit was introduced to service on the Oxted line in 1962, seeing use on services between London Victoria and Uckfield and from Eridge to Tonbridge via Tunbridge Wells. Services from East Grinstead to Horsted Keynes and Haywards Heath via the Ardingly line would have been operated by 2-BIL electric units.

PART 4

Electric Multiple Units

Class 405 4-SUB
These 4-car Suburban (4-SUB) EMUs reached their zenith in their use throughout Southern Suburbia. They were a direct result of the Southern Region in 1948, at the formation of the nationalised British Railways, taking over the largest live third rail network in Britain. The mainstay of the Southern Region's scheme for supplying adequate trains to meet the needs of the London commuters was this fleet of high density slam door units of all-steel construction. They were designed by O.V.S. Bulleid, Chief Mechanical Engineer of the Southern Railway until nationalisation. When delivered they would have carried the malachite green worn by 4732 in preservation. Initially the new units were supplied with compartments, but others were built as saloons with central corridors. Slam doors accessed each of the interior seating bays which facilitated fast boarding and disembarkation. All of the 4-SUB units were capable of working in multiple with each other, and also

Lewes, Saturday, 10 August 1991: Class 405 4-SUB 4732 arrives with the 10.29 Seaford to Brighton.

with other Southern EMU fleets which gave the Southern Region much flexibility in operations and equipment. They proved a very familiar site around the traditional Southern commuter territory south of the Thames and their operational routes included north Kent, Surrey and Sussex, Middlesex and Hampshire. They were frequently used on busy summer weekends for trips to Brighton and the South Coast seaside resorts along with race meetings and other highlight events. The preserved 4-SUB No. 4732 was built at British Rail's Eastleigh Carriage Works in 1951 and was one of the last batch of SUBs to be constructed.

Class 411 4-CEP

This timber signal box was built by the South Eastern and Chatham Railway in 1901. It formerly straddled the lines between London Bridge and Blackfriars and was to be reused at Canterbury West where it was reassembled in 1927 and took over the functions of the two South Eastern Railway cabins in January 1928. It was suspended at height on a lattice gantry at the north end of the station where it offered a clear view over the trainshed roofs. Its 72-lever frame of the Hallam & Sykes design, with a type of frame which was jointly patented by the South Eastern and Chatham Railway, is now much reduced although still in use. It is listed by English Heritage.

Canterbury West, Friday, 27 July 2001: Class 411/5 4-CEP 1614 in NSE livery departs north past the 'off' lower quadrant semaphore signal, running as empty coaching stock to the stabling sidings early afternoon.

The third rail direct current system was adopted in south east England due to the relatively low cost of installation, removing the need for overhead gantries supporting catenary collection of the current, and avoiding the obstruction of the visual sighting of signals. The Class 411 EMUs were designed as Express Passenger units and could reach 90mph. Designated 4-CEP (4-Car Corridor layout Electro-Pneumatic) and built in 1956 by Eastleigh, this Kent Coast fleet was refurbished in the first half of the 1980s. This saw the Class provided with Commonwealth bogies which certainly offered a steady and comfortable ride.

Quite what visitors to the UK from the Continent made of antiquated BR Standard design, Mk 1 based, EMUs – and even more so of the Southern's slam door stock also used on some of the expresses from Kent's ports to London – as their first acquaintance with Britain's Railways in the new millennium we can merely speculate. The fading Network SouthEast paintwork also tells its own story, although there is at least a lack of graffiti which tended to ravage the train fleets of German, French and most dramatically Italian Railways where the original operator's livery was completely covered by that which some consider to be art!

On the next page is a reminder that these electric units' operations on the south east division were not limited to the main line to Dover/Ramsgate and Canterbury but also made regular appearances on the Strood to Maidstone West and Paddock Wood branch and on the Sittingbourne to Sheerness-on-Sea shuttles, which therefore

Canterbury East, Tuesday, 1 August 2000: Class 411/5 3-CEP 1115, in NSE livery, forming the 15.51 departure, 15.23 from Dover Priory, to London Victoria.

offered a high quality of travel for these comparatively quiet branch lines! This scene captures both the traditional railway atmosphere and that of the local industry demonstrated by this historic paper mill. Kent's Medway Valley has a long tradition of paper making and the Townsend Hook Paper Mill seen here is one of the largest mills still in existence along the valley, and dates back in its present form to the 1820s. No doubt the station here provided the hub of transport for those who commuted in from Maidstone and North Kent to work here, and perhaps still caters for this demand today.

Interestingly, as part of the publicity provided by Network SouthEast in 1989, plans were made public for electrification of some of the few remaining routes in the Southern area which had evaded such. These included Ashford to Hastings, Hurst Green to Uckfield and Reading to Salisbury via Basingstoke. None of these has been achieved to date, bi-mode trains equipped with batteries now being most likely to be provided for the Ashford to Hastings 'Marshlink' although third rail electrification remains a possibility for this and the Uckfield line.

In the mid-1980s the railway from Tonbridge to Hastings was singled through Somerhill, Strawberry Hill and Wadhurst Tunnels

Snodland, Friday, 31 October 1997: Class 411 4-CEP 1580 departs over the level crossing and past the signal box with the 15.03 Strood to Maidstone West.

Battle, Saturday, 28 July 2001: Class 411/5 4-CEP 1607 in somewhat grubby NSE livery departs with the 14.51 Hastings to London Charing Cross.

to permit, once fully electrified, standard width EMUs to operate the route from Hastings to Tonbridge. Electrification started in July 1984 and the full electric timetable along the route was commenced in May 1986. The legacy of this, however, is that when a train runs late in either direction, then inevitably there are implications for trains passing in the opposite direction which must wait for each other at either side of the single line sections.

The Kent Coast express rolling stock was the culmination of the development of the 4-COR units introduced for the 1937 Portsmouth electrification but using electro-pneumatic brakes and BR standard carriage designs. The units were of two types, one incorporating a buffet car. Buffet units were designated 4-BEP and the remainder of the fleet designated 4-CEP. These 4-CEP units had a Motor Brake Second Open, with the driving position in the cabs at each end of the unit, and with a Trailer Composite and Trailer Second as intermediate vehicles; in the 4-BEP units the Trailer Second coach was replaced by a Trailer Buffet. English Electric 250 hp EE507 traction motors supplied the power. In the 4-BEPs the kitchen equipment comprised an electric cooker with a grill and

Paddock Wood, Friday, 31 October 1997: Class 411 4-CEP 1565 arrives with the 13.20 Maidstone West, 13.40 Paddock Wood to Three Bridges.

hot food closet, a refrigerator and a freezer (for keeping ice creams). Water used for catering purposes was carried in a 120 gallon tank mounted on the underframe of the carriage.

Maintenance depots for the units were Stewarts Lane – the centre for driver training – and Ashford, where the new Chart Leacon depot was constructed on the south side of the Tonbridge line just under a mile from the station. In time, Ramsgate became established as their main depot.

In the mid-1970s, it became apparent that the fleet of 4-CEP and 4-BEP units would need an extension to their anticipated 25 years, of up to 40 years. Their Mk 1 interiors were very much a first generation design and their standard of accommodation had become decidedly aged. Swindon Works was allocated their extensive refurbishment which was undertaken between 1980 and 1984. The refurbishment included fitting new seating of a type used in the BR Mk 2 e/f hauled stock, and improved lighting to the saloons. Double-glazed windows were fitted whilst the sliding ventilators were retained and an improved heating system implemented. Units were reformed with the DMBSOs

Eastleigh, Saturday, 16 October 1999: Class 411/5 4-CEP 1534, ex-Kent Coast express stock, arrives to form the 12.40 Eastleigh to Southampton Central.

reformed as DMSO (Driving Motor Second Open) with the guard's section converted into an extra eight-seat bay, the TSK replaced by a TSOL (Trailer Second Open Lavatory) with a saloon replacing compartments, and the TC became a TBCK (Trailer Brake Composite Corridor) in which the Guard's brake section replaced second class compartments. New Commonwealth bogies ensured a more comfortable ride. The refurbished units carried the standard four digit number as seen in the units portrayed in this section.

At privatisation in 1996, many of the surviving eighty-five CEP units in service were swiftly withdrawn or transferred to the South West area, such as this unit which was based at Fratton at the time of the photograph.

Class 415 4-EPB and Class 416 2-EPB

In some ways the photograph opposite summarises the typical Southern inner suburban train scenario that greeted London's commuters and photographers alike in the mid-1980s – a grey day with the standard blue and grey BR livery slam door stock, multitudes of which pottered around the intricate network of the Southern's many interlacing main line and branch line rails. The

ELECTRIC MULTIPLE UNITS • 129

4-EPB (Electro Pneumatic Brake) units were a direct descendent to the Class 405 4-SUB, and were built at Eastleigh. The set formations were also similar to the later-built 4-SUB units, comprising a Driving Motor Brake Second, Trailer Second Compartment and Trailer Second Open and a further Driving Motor Brake Second. They were capable of working in multiple with each other, and they were compatible with other Southern EMU fleets. The Class 415s survived as long as they did partly thanks to the fact that they were built without use of blue asbestos insulation (used in more modern vehicles) - and it was economically attractive to keep these units running, as maintenance and spare parts were not a difficulty.

Crystal Palace Low Level started as an LB&SCR terminus in 1854. It stood at the end of a short spur from Sydenham on the London Bridge to Croydon line and became a through station when connected to the west of London via the West End and Crystal Palace Railway in 1856. An eastward connection was made to Norwood Junction in 1858 and the West End and Crystal

Holborn Viaduct, Monday, 13 April 1987: left, Class 415/2 4-EPB 5315 awaits a driver and imminent departure with the 13.58 service to Sevenoaks, and right, Class 415/4 Class 415 4-EPBs 5422 and 5453 are stabled empty coaching stock.

Crystal Palace, Saturday, 6 June 1987: Class 415/4 4-EPB 5443 departs with the 17.44 to London Bridge, 17.35 from East Croydon.

Palace Railway was extended to Beckenham Junction. Following completion of the 746-yd Crystal Palace Tunnel, through trains to Clapham Junction were introduced, routed via West Norwood and Streatham Hill. In the 1980s, the station entrance received investment in the form of a new glazed ticket hall which recalls the original Crystal Palace's arched roof structure (seen directly above the train in this photograph). In 2002 Railtrack spent a cool £4 million refurbishing the station which included significant work on the roof and refurbishment of office space on the top floor. It helped give a brighter and more spacious atmosphere to the station, situated as it is in a cutting.

The global problem that poses a challenge to any railway operator faced with a need to provide space for rush hour stock, or in the cases of many of the large seaside resorts for the summer peak Saturdays excursion and relief trains, is finding appropriate provision for their stabling. In the case of the latter this could involve requiring use of sidings many miles away from the resort's terminus, in the case of the former it is a little easier in terms of distance from the city apart from the need to start moving stock out of the relevant sidings during the afternoon lull in this case. Even so, a distance of just under 14 miles from Charing Cross or 15 miles from Victoria is still significant and must require some

ELECTRIC MULTIPLE UNITS • **131**

keen organisation of ensuring trains are in the right place at the right time during the evening peak.

It was 28 February 1926 when full electric services were introduced from Charing Cross and Cannon Street to the Mid Kent line, and to Bromley North and Orpington. For both the 2-EPB and 4-EPB units, they would be in service from the 1950s right through until the era of Network SouthEast, with the South Eastern and Central division seeing their withdrawal by 1991.

In the photograph of Tattenham Corner station is a reminder that the Southern's main line and branch line traffic required fleets of third rail units to be versatile and capable of meeting the need to move large numbers for weekday morning and evening rush hours from the city, and also for sporting events such as horse racing – at Epsom or Ascot – and for rugby and football at Twickenham. Consequently, timetables for weekdays and weekends needed to be planned to provide frequent services with as few changes of train required as financially viable.

This was also a time of transition with the railway infrastructure, where rationalisation saw disused yards and sidings removed, their

Orpington Station, Tuesday, 31 May 1988: A view over the southern end of the station featuring the signal box and sidings containing rush-hour stock. Left: Class 416/2 2-EPB 6205, 415/4 4-EPB 5480 and 415/1 4-EPB 5230, all based at Slade Green; Right: Class 415/4 EPB 5485 departs with the 13.02 to London Charing Cross.

Tattenham Corner, Saturday, 30 July 1988: left to right, Class 415/4 4-EPB 5439, Class 455 5819 (in NSE colours) and Class 415/4 4-EPB 5450. Rails are evidently removed from trackbed serving the disused left hand platforms and centre roads, where race traffic specials had once held sway.

lack of use reflecting the preference by race-attendees, for example, to use fast motorways and private cars to reach their chosen destinations. It was also the start of the introduction of new second generation purpose-designed and built suburban electric units with automatic opening doors, wide aisles and effective heating. The powered vehicle was now within the middle of the formation although without any guard's accommodation which would now occupy the rear cab. The Class 455s were introduced between 1982 and 1985 and offered a much improved quality of ride as well as greater reliability. They were, however, incompatible with other designs of electric units and were therefore restricted to multiple operation within their own class. The straight-lined and angular NSE livery suited them well.

Here's an iconic location for a railway photograph. Built at Eastleigh in 1953-56 to the same general design of the 4-EPBs, the same refurbishment applied to the latter was extended to these units from 1979 onwards until 1986. Built for the London Waterloo to Windsor and Weybridge services, they also saw use on the

ELECTRIC MULTIPLE UNITS • **133**

south eastern division where they were used in conjunction with pairs of Class 4-EPBs to strengthen train lengths to ten cars in order to ease serious overcrowding. The units were allocated BR TOPS class number 413 in 1972, this being amended to class 416 in 1975 and revised to 416/2 subsequently, from July 1984 when all units previously numbered in the 57xx series were renumbered in the 62xx series. Thus in this photograph 6237 was previously 5737, withdrawn 7 November 1994, and 6271 was previously 5771, withdrawn 4 May 1994.

Blackfriars station saw investment with new and longer platforms constructed during the new year of 2011. These enabled it to accommodate 12-car trains and stretched right across Blackfriars Bridge. New bay platforms were also constructed on the western side of the bridge.

Just evident at Vauxhall station is another iconic London landmark – Westminster Palace – seen on the far right. In some ways these 2-EPB and 4-EPB units had in due course of time become an icon in their own right. The Tyneside third rail system

Blackfriars, Monday, 13 April 1987: Class 416/2 2-EPB units 6237 and 6271 at platform; Tower Bridge in the background right.

Vauxhall Station, Friday, 29 July 1994: Class 416 2-EPB Route Learning Unit 931001, formed of Departmental Unit 977856 and 977857, ex-6401, passes en route for Waterloo International and operating over CTL International lines. It was based at Stewarts Lane Depot.

saw fifteen 4-EPBs (similar to the BR Southern units apart from a larger guard's section) placed in service until 1963 when that system was de-electrified and that stock made redundant and transferred to the Southern to operate alongside their stock of the same Class.

Class 419 MLV

This rolling stock was unique to the Southern in that these ten motor luggage vans were built for use in continental boat trains, providing capacity for passengers' luggage and for mail which was carried under the Customs seal. The alternative of attaching standard vans at the rear of the Kent Coast Express services was ruled out because of its adverse effect on the power-to-weight ratio of the electric units. Also, such vans would be ineffective as they would be traditionally marshalled at the London end of the boat trains but lacked a driving position. The steep gradient of the Folkestone Harbour branch would also raise problems.

The MLVs were introduced from 1958 (the two MLVs seen here) and 1960/61. They were supplied with two English Electric EE507

250hp traction motors (similar to the 4-CEPs and 4-BEPs with which they worked) and also with traction batteries for use on non-electrified sections. Such was necessary for the port quaysides where use of a live third rail was not possible for safety reasons, as this was where the luggage and mail was unloaded and loaded. They were formed of a small guard's compartment and two luggage compartments, one a third longer than the other. Each MLV could haul tail loads comprising vans of up to 100 tons (50 tons on the Folkestone Harbour branch). They were not provided with gangway connections for mail and luggage security reasons. These MLVs were occasionally used in traffic within normal mail train duties on the Eastern and Central divisions of the Southern.

The two units are seen in the two liveries concurrent at the time of the photograph – one in 'Jaffa Cake' brown, beige and orange which was also applied to some of the 4-CEPs, and one in BR blue and grey.

Dover Priory, Wednesday, 10 August 1988: Class 419 MLVs 9001/9002, 68001 and 68002, stabled.

Class 421 4-CIG and Class 422 4-BIG
These comfortable electric units conveyed passengers bound for the Isle of Wight with a convenient connection at Lymington Pier. The carriage windows on these comfortable trains provided a view of the passing landscape uncompromised by intrusive pillars found on some modern units. The 1964-built Express passenger trains, based

Lymington, Friday, 7 August 1987: Class 421 4-CIG 1250 crosses Lymington viaduct, between Lymington Pier and Town, with the 12.57 Lymington Pier to Brockenhurst. Owing to power supply limitations on the Lymington branch, 4-REP with 4-TC stock could not be used, with 4-CIG units providing the requisite stock instead.

on the Mk.1 coaching stock design, featured an improved much neater front end design with rounded corners between the front, bodysides and roof. The Corridor Intermediate Guard acronym (4-CIG) was designated to these multiple units. The Driving Trailer Composites (DTC) of these units were equipped with third rail collecting shoes with the electricity transferred to the motor coach via a traction cable running the length of the train. By late 1965 the whole fleet was in service replacing the 4-COR (Corridor) electric units on the direct Portsmouth services as well as seeing use on London Victoria to south coast resorts such as Brighton and Littlehampton. In the early 1980s they could sometimes be found working on the Reading to London Waterloo services where they provided a higher level of comfort as compared to the 4-VEP units. On the South Eastern division, in the summer of 1991 two batches were transferred by Network SouthEast from Brighton to Ramsgate and these were dedicated to the Charing Cross to Hastings services, including at least one daily service routed to Ramsgate via Tonbridge.

Built in 1965, the Class 422 4-BIG (Buffet Brighton) units were distinguished from the 4-CIGs (Corridor Brighton) by the inclusion of a Trailer Buffet Second. As many as two Class 421s combined with a Class 422 formed busier services and, joined by a gangway,

ELECTRIC MULTIPLE UNITS • **137**

passengers from all parts of the train could reach the buffet coach in these 4-BIG units. Like the Class 421, they had bogies designated B5(S) which gave a ride which was even better than the renowned Commonwealth Bogies still sought by preservation railways, being highly praised for their steady and firm riding qualities. They were refurbished in the mid-1980s when their blue asbestos was

Left and below:
First picture: Lewes, Saturday, 10 August 1991: Class 422/1 4-BIG 1734 departs with the 09.51 London Victoria to Hastings via Lewes. Second picture: Lewes Station, Tuesday, 25 July 1995: Class 422 4-BIG 2203 departs past the signal box with the 18.54 Brighton to Hastings. Note on the far left are the remains of the Down loop.

Fareham, Wallington Viaduct, Sunday, 11 October 1998: A Class 423 4-VEP in Network SouthEast livery is seen operating the 12.47 Portsmouth Harbour to Southampton Central. It crosses the estuary of the little Wallington River, where it flows into a corner of Portsmouth Harbour.

removed. As seen in these two photographs, the Network South-East livery suited them well. Some of the South Eastern division units which found later use on South Central wore the 'Jaffa Cake' brown, beige and orange livery.

Class 423 4-VEP

Eastleigh depot acquired an allocation of Class 4-CIG and 4-VEP EMUs by 1990 when parts of the depot were equipped with third rail. This allocation was part of a plan, reversed in 1994, to close Fratton depot. It is intriguing to note that Eastleigh depot would come to see much use in providing wagon repairs, fuelling of a range of locomotives and even overnight servicing of CrossCountry 'Voyagers'.

The Class 423 4-VEP (Vestibule Electro-Pneumatic Brake) units were defined by their designation which referred to them being gangwayed throughout with vestibules, hence 'Vestibuled EPB'. Built at York, these were introduced in 1967 for semi-fast services, powered by the same English Electric EE507 250hp traction motors also used in the 4-CEPs and 4-BEPs, 4-CIGs and 4-BIGs. Bodywork design was also similar to the latter units although they were high-density with consequently a larger number of seats as compared to the Express units. They had side doors to each of the seating bays in order to facilitate fast boarding and disembarking. The Class was dedicated to the Waterloo to Bournemouth main line, allocated to the new Bournemouth EMU depot, and also formed most of the semi-fast services from Waterloo to Reading. They were intended for semi-fast services in the outer-suburban areas of the Central and South West Divisions although some did find employment in the South Eastern division as well. Some 4-VEPs were also dedicated to the London Victoria to Gatwick Airport service. These were modified for such, provided with a larger amount of room for luggage created by the removal of some seating. 'Rapid City Link' special logos were inscribed on these trains accompanied by a framed silhouette of an aircraft. The units were built with a large guard's van area in the motor coach. After the parcels and mail business diminished, it was decided to convert part of this area into two seating bays, and such work was carried out at Eastleigh Works in the 1990s.

The Class 423 survived until the end of EMU slam-door stock in November 2005. Several vehicles from the Class have been preserved, including the celebrity set 3417 *Gordon Pettitt* which received a repaint by South West Trains into its BR blue livery to commemorate the final months in traffic of the slam-door fleet, this unit being selected as it was one of those which had the longest life expectancy. It is preserved and owned by the Southern Electric Traction Group and resides at Strawberry Hill depot.

Of additional interest is third rail powered 4VEP's resemblance to and looking just as good as a 4-TC, see page 140. The 'TC' designation stands for Trailer Corridor which was used for locomotive-hauled units of three, four, six and seven fixed formation sets with a driving cab at each end (though not equipped with push-pull controls). When first introduced, the 4-TCs appeared in overall rail blue livery with small yellow warning panels and with small aluminium BR arrows affixed below their side cab windows, as also perfectly demonstrated here by 4-VEP 3417. The yellow warning panels were subsequently enlarged to cover the whole cab front. The 4-TCs and 4-VEPS were repainted during the early 1970s into BR blue and grey, at the same time losing their aluminium arrows in the process. Alongside their use with the London to Bournemouth trains, the 4-TC sets also saw

Corfe Castle Station, Swanage Railway, Sunday, 11 May 2008: Class 423 4-VEP 3417 in immaculate BR blue, here seen featuring as hauled stock for the 16.30 Norden to Swanage. Right: stabled in the Up siding, Class 117 Pressed Steel Suburban 3-car DMU (51346, 51388, 59516) preserved on the Swanage Railway.

use on Portsmouth to Cardiff Class 33 hauled services, along with those from Salisbury to both Reading and Portsmouth – often linked with Salisbury to London Waterloo duties.

Class 483

Petrol engine Drewry railcars once ran on the pier tramway seen rusting away on the left. Journey time was short, which is just as well as passengers would have had to endure the wooden slatted seats provided, with hanging straps available for the standees. Restricted to their own tracks, bizarrely they could only be driven from one end, being reversed up the pier with the assistance of a countdown marker device in the cab when approaching the Pier Head.

The tradition of London Transport supplying second hand ex-Underground trains for the light railway that served the Isle of Wight third rail electrified line to Shanklin in 1967, when the Class 485 and 486 units were delivered, was repeated in 1989-90 when 28 Metro-Cammell built 1938 vintage tube stock coaches were shipped over for replacing the former units. Each of the ten 2-car sets rebuilt at Eastleigh was fitted with four Crompton Parkinson/GEC/BTH traction motors which provided the requisite power for these lightweight units. The 'Island Line' was operated by Stagecoach in the privatisation era, and by South West Trains when the line was re-franchised. London Transport red livery was applied as the standard livery from 2007. They were finally retired after 82 years' service in 2021.

In a substantial upgrade in 2021 the line benefited from investment funded by the DfT, Solent Local Enterprise Partnership and the Isle of Wight Council. Ryde St Johns depot was renovated to accommodate a new fleet of trains, also high-tech software for the maintenance of the fleet. New signalling equipment was supplied and a new loop developed at Brading to accommodate improved frequency of half-hourly trains, with enhanced connections with the Wightlink ferries. Ryde pier also received treatment to prolong the life of the listed structure. Late delivery of the new Class 484s caused by complex software issues meant that it was November 2021 before the new trains, formed of former London Transport Underground stock extensively refurbished by Vivarail in Long Marston, were at last introduced to service.

Note the station canopies, semaphore signals and signal box, all reminiscent of an earlier era. The Island Line's depot is evident to

Ryde Pier, Sunday, 9 July 1995: Class 483 units 006 and 007 slow in their approach to Ryde Pier Head station.

Ryde St John's Road, Wednesday, 27 May 1992: Class 483 483007 departs with the 12.08 to Shanklin, while on the right 483002 prepares to depart with the 12.10 to Ryde Pier Head.

the left. The Isle of Wight Railway Company's motif can be seen in the canopy spandrels. The signal box was previously in use at London Waterloo East. It was moved to the Island in 1928, and at the time of the photograph controlled the whole of the Island Line, as Brading and Sandown signal boxes were abolished in 1989.

PART 5

Departmental and Civil Engineers' Trains

Class 930 and Class 931 Departmental Electric Units
It may be a gloomy February day but the mundane everyday railway performs its routine day in, day out without ceremony or fanfare. This elderly unit may well have been in recent use during the cold nights of mid-winter keeping the third rail from icing over – an essential aspect for the morning's rush-hour trains to operate smoothly – but even as a veteran it is still earning its keep. Departmental trains

Fratton, Monday, 17 February 1986: De-icing Unit 012 Class 930 930012 formed of DB975605 and DB975604, ex-4-SUB 4377 driving motor coaches, stabled at the side of the depot. It was later renumbered 930001. This was finally withdrawn in 2002. The EMU depot was opened in 1937 alongside the steam shed, which closed in 1959 and is now the site of a retail park. Class 444 and 450 have since been stabled here at the Train Care Depot.

across Europe often include historic rolling stock, providing a fascinating glimpse into long-departed train designs.

Advantages of using the dc third rail electrification system are primarily that it is most economic to install, as compared to overhead wiring, and no resiting of signals is required. The dc electric traction motor favoured by the Southern proved itself sturdy and reliable. The power to weight ratio of EMUs is beneficial, with all space in the stock available for seating or luggage.

However, ice and snow, along with autumnal leaf mulch, causes problems and requires application of de-icing agent or high pressure water jets to assist train adhesion. Such requires regular diagrams overnight and during the day of such departmental trains as this to combat these weather related challenges. When converted, these de-icing and rail cleaning units were fitted with various different types of equipment including new live rail scrapers, marker lights and electric train supply connections.

London Waterloo, Saturday, 1 October 1988: On display nearest: De-icing and Sandite unit Class 930 930007, DB 975593 and DB 975592, ex-4-SUB 4127/4604, based at Gillingham EMU depot. This Class 931 was rebuilt in 1979 and withdrawn in 2002. To its rear, Class EM/2 27000 *Electra* owned by the West Yorkshire Transport Museum at this time, in Brunswick green livery. Behind that is Class 71 E5001 (71001) belonging to the NRM.

DEPARTMENTAL AND CIVIL ENGINEERS' TRAINS • 145

London Victoria carriage holding sidings, also known as Grosvenor Road Carriage Sidings, Wednesday, 14 April 1999: left: Class 423 4-VEP 3422 in Connex livery; centre: Sandite unit Class 931 931001, ex-Class 416/4 2-EPB 6232/6401, DB977856 and DB977857; right: Class 411 4-CEP 1511 in NSE livery - all based at Ramsgate depot.

Variety is the spice of life! This epithet is applicable to these rather different design units and even in the liveries seen here, with 3422 wearing the white with yellow lower body version of the Connex livery. The Class 931 was withdrawn in 2002. It was rebuilt from its 2-EPB design in 1993 as a route instruction set with the original headcode box removed and two additional windows installed in the cab front, presumably at the rear of this unit as seen here. It acted as a viewing saloon and classroom, including in 1994 when it was used in daily runs between Waterloo International and Dollands Moor providing training for UK and French drivers for Eurostar operations along the route initially taken to the Channel Tunnel.

Civil Engineers' Trains

Somewhat unsung, partly because they work especially at night or on lines 'closed for engineering' it is worth including a couple of examples of the multi-million pound machines which facilitate the specialist engineers that keep the railway infrastructure in a suitable condition to allow the freight and passenger trains that use the permanent way to proceed in safety and efficiency. Replacing

Tonbridge, Friday, 13 October 2023: One of the small fleet of rail grinding machines passes through the station.

worn rails, installing new points at junctions, dealing with flooding or drainage, extending the life of viaducts in bleak landscapes, the list is long and the training required provides a career which rewards well but demands professionalism and determination. Machines such as this incorporate highly technical equipment requiring a high level of skill in their operation. They assist meeting appropriate time schedules to complete the necessary work safely and precisely.

The rail-grinding trains maintain the track thereby extending the life of the rail. These trains remove small layers of metal from the railhead which helps keep the track in good condition. Able to grind at speeds of up to 15mph they can travel at speeds of up to 70mph between the various engineering sites on the network, which means they don't hold up faster passenger and freight trains when en route. The machines are modular and can be attached together to make larger machines, which assists the replacement of parts and components, reducing the down time of the machine when requiring repairs and maintenance. They are equipped with an obstacle avoidance system to limit the impact of trackside furniture and equipment when in use.

Railhead Treatment Trains can be observed at work across the country especially during the leaf fall season. They are particularly needed on Southern electrified routes with third rail supply. Autumn trees may be colourful but when their leaves fall onto the rails they are consequently ground in by passing trains, thus creating a mulch which leaves a layer of slippery paste on the running rails. This can create problems when trains brake for stations or speed restrictions, with resultant wheel slip – and this similarly applies to trains when they accelerate away.

The high pressure water jets help to remove this sludge while applying a mix of gel, sand and steel or iron pellets which further assist train adhesion. The MPVs (Multi-Purpose Vehicles), as shown here, and locomotive hauled RHTTs where longer distances apply, are an important and essential part of Network Rail's strategy for containing this seasonal challenge. Operators of RHTTs within the UK include many of the freight operating companies, including GBRf, Colas Rail Freight, DB Cargo, DRS (Direct Rail Services), and Freightliner.

Otford, Sunday, 15 October 2023: Railhead Treatment Train DR 98930 passes through this atmospheric station carrying out its spraying as it heads north.

PART 6

Second Generation Electric Multiple Units

Class 313
These BREL York Suburban 3-car EMUs were built in 1976, and initially provided services on local services within the Great Northern's London area of the Eastern Region, operating from an overhead power supply. They were also equipped for third rail to facilitate their use of London Moorgate, and required their dual-voltage equipment as the tunnels situated beyond Drayton Park were too narrow for overhead catenary wires to be fitted. They could therefore operate from 25kV ac overhead and from 750V dc third rail.

As part of a major upgrade to the Coastway services radiating from Brighton, nineteen spare Class 313 sets were transferred to Southern in 2010, replacing more modern Class 377s previously used on the route but required for main-line services. They were modified for this purpose, with only the dc equipment left in

Worthing, Tuesday, 3 April 2012: Southern Class 313/2 313205 is at platform with the 10.26 to Brighton, 09.29 ex- Portsmouth Harbour, 'Coastway' service.

place, and the 25Kv ac pantograph removed. These were then renumbered in the Class 313/2 series. More recently they were becoming increasingly unreliable – and their lack of on-board toilets reinforced their unpopularity in view of some long journey times incurred by passengers travelling along the coast. Recalcitrant units were despatched to Brighton Depot for repairs. The resulting shortages of stock consequently saw cancellations and withdrawals are under way at the time of writing.

Class 350

Raising some eyebrows among the enthusiasts at Clapham Junction, four of these dual-voltage EMUs, equipped for 25Kv ac and 750V dc, were used to operate Southern's Milton Keynes to East Croydon service for three months in 2009. This was a result of Southern loaning eight of its Class 377/2s to First Capital Connect owing to late delivery of their new Bombardier Class 377/5s. They had entered service in this capacity on 16 March and remained in such use until mid-June. Class 350 350114 and 350112 also featured in this exchange. Appearance of these units in full LMR colours south of the Thames certainly offered an unusual addition to the spectrum of the usual diet at Clapham!

Clapham Junction, Tuesday, 26 May 2009: LMR Siemens Desiro UK Class 350/1 350123 operating an early p.m. north-bound ecs (probably driver training).

Class 375 'Electrostar'

With no need for safety concerns with slam doors thanks to their powered sliding doors or even about fitting the restricted gauge of the Tonbridge to Hastings route, these units have settled in well to their diagrams along this lengthy route to the south coast. Equipped with two Adtranz asynchronous traction motors of 250kW (335hp) in both Driving Motor Standard Opens (DMSO) and capable of 100mph, they were first regularly deployed in Kent with Connex South Eastern during the summer timetable of 2001 on services between London Victoria and Ramsgate. Fitted with regenerative braking, they generate electricity when decelerating and this is beneficial in powering the trains' electric motors and returning that electricity to the grid.

These Class 375/6 units are equipped with a pantograph carried by the Pantograph Trailer Standard Open (PTSO). The associated electrical equipment required for 25Kv operation means they have dual-voltage capacity. With power available from the traction motors as referred to, the power output of 2,010hp is just over twice that of the 4-CEP and 4-VEP units, given their power -to- weight ratio of c.11hp per tonne.

Although these units have a potential for 100mph running, they rarely are given the chance to exceed 90mph and that is most likely when operating the semi-fast service to Margate and Ramsgate along the 26-mile section of straight line that runs between Tonbridge and

Sevenoaks, Saturday, 14 October 2023: Southeastern Class 375/7 'Electrostar' 375710 departs with the 09.21 Hastings to London Charing Cross.

SECOND GENERATION ELECTRIC MULTIPLE UNITS • 151

Wadhurst, Friday, 3 September 2021: Southeastern Class 375/6 'Electrostar' 375614 departs from this characterful East Sussex station with the 09.21 Hastings to London Charing Cross.

Hastings, Friday, 3 September 2021: right, Southeastern Class 375/6 'Electrostar' 375628 will form the 10.50 to London Charing Cross, and left Class 375/9 'Electrostar' 375902 awaits departure with the 10.32 to London Charing Cross.

Ashford. This was possible at the time when the train was divided at Tonbridge and the front unit ran fast to Ashford. The Class 375/9 is equipped only for third rail 750V dc. The fleet of Class 375s was given a £10 million upgrade throughout 2023, which included fitting at-seat USB points, new LED lighting and energy metering. This was carried out at Southeastern's Ashford Train Maintenance

Minster, Saturday, 14 October 2023: Class 375/8 'Electrostar' 375817 forms the rear set of the 13.29 service to Ramsgate from London Charing Cross and passes Minster West Signal box.

Centre. LED lighting uses 75-80 per cent less energy compared to incandescent or fluorescent lights, helping towards reducing greenhouse gas emissions.

The single- track spur branching off to the right to the line from Ramsgate to Margate via Sandwich and Deal is used by a couple of daily services at the time of writing, the 07.05 Faversham to Ashford (reverses at Minster) and the 15.24 Dover to Faversham (reverses at Minster), and also for a very limited number of empty coaching stock moves. Previously a double track junction, it was singled in 1981. The signal box dates from 1929 and is of Southern Railway design and hints at the architecture of former signalling contractors Saxby & Farmer. The associated impressive double-armed semaphore signal brackets were replaced by three-aspect colour lights. The original divergence point of the Deal spur was nearer the crossover points alongside the signal box, but this was changed during the rationalisation of the layout in 1981. There was also a bay line to the right of the Up platform, which was removed at the same time, having long been out of use.

Class 376 'Electrostar'

Built in 2004/5, these units are equipped with two Bombardier asynchronous traction motors of 250kW (335hp) thus sharing the same power as the Class 375. They are in many ways similar to their 'Networker' Class 365 and are not fitted with central gangways to connect passenger areas of coupled units, and their maximum

SECOND GENERATION ELECTRIC MULTIPLE UNITS • 153

***Left and below**:* **London Cannon** Street, Friday, 15 January 2016: Contrasting views of Class 376 'Electrostar' units somewhat lost amidst the classic and modern architecture of the surrounding buildings of the City of London.

Wandsworth Common, Saturday, 14 May 2005: Two Class 377/1 'Electrostar' Southern express/outer suburban 4-car EMUs with 377163 at the rear, in Southern livery, pass with a London bound service in the early afternoon.

speed of 75mph is considered appropriate in view of their frequent stop/start at stations which are of suburban rather than longer distances. Their intended use has been for North Kent, including Charing Cross to Orpington and the Hayes branch, both of which saw the trains introduced from May 2004.

Impressionistic modernistic architecture of office space with surrounding buildings seen at the top of page 153, has resulted in their earning status in their own right. These include the Cheesegrater named so by its distinctive wedge shape and tapered glass facade. Partly hidden is the Gherkin, a bullet-shaped skyscraper with diamond shaped windows, constructed by the renowned architect Norman Foster who provided the design for the redevelopment of London St Pancras station. To the right, behind the cranes, is 20 Fenchurch Street, known as the Walkie Talkie, resembling a 1980s mobile phone. In the second picture looking west are the more traditional icons of St Paul's Cathedral and Cannon Street station's two Grade II listed towers facing the Thames, remnants from the original station that was opened in 1863.

Class 377 'Electrostar'

Constructed by Bombardier and introduced to service from May 2003, these units share a similar traction package to the Class 375. They are equipped with eight pick-up shoes, twice the number

SECOND GENERATION ELECTRIC MULTIPLE UNITS • 155

of previous generation 4-car EMUs, which enables them to ride smoothly over most third-rail gaps. The main stamping ground for this sub-class use is the Brighton main line and routes serving south London; they replaced the 4-CIG and 4-VEP units. They are fully air-conditioned which during their earliest years in service caused problems with the consequential higher power consumption which resulted in significant upgrades to the 750V dc third rail power supply being necessary.

Here in mid-Sussex, almost in South Downs territory, it is easy from this photograph to see why tree growth can cause such problems when it comes to the annual shedding of their leaves in the autumn, with the requirement to use the Railhead Treatment Trains as previously featured.

Balcombe is famed for its 450m long viaduct, positioned between Haywards Heath and Balcombe stations, which was built to facilitate the London to Brighton Railway to span the valley of the River Ouse, thereby connecting the Sussex coast to the capital. Completed in 1842, it is said that the viaduct contains around 11 million bricks, and is 97ft (29m) high, carried on 37 semi-circular arches and surmounted by balustrades. A Grade II listed building, it underwent restoration in the late 1990s to restore it to its former glory. Its massive features and aesthetically magnificent proportions mean that its presence enhances the landscape within the valley of the Ouse.

Balcombe, Monday, 2 April 2012: Southern Class 377/1 'Electrostar' 377132 (based at Brighton depot) with an early afternoon service for London Victoria.

The Brighton main line remains as important as ever, with fastest services scheduled to complete the journey to and from London Victoria in just under an hour. Brighton's popularity as an all-year round resort justifies the high frequency of trains from London as well as the south coast.

Right and below:
First picture: Balcombe, Monday, 2 April 2012: Southern Class 377/1 'Electrostar' 377144 passes with an early afternoon southbound fast service from London Victoria. Second picture: Gatwick Airport, Friday, 29 May 2009: Southern Class 377/1 'Electrostar' 377105 arrives with an early afternoon service from London Victoria to Brighton.

SECOND GENERATION ELECTRIC MULTIPLE UNITS • **157**

Apart from a limited number of freight trains such as that from Hanwell Bridge Loop to Purley Foster Yeoman, the line is now passenger dedicated, especially with the much increased role that Gatwick Airport now provides in comparison to June 1958 when it was opened by Queen Elizabeth II. Since then, passenger use has grown from 186,000 to over 40 million passengers.

These were three ex-Southern Class 377/2s that transferred to First Capital Connect in 2011. Other Class 377/2 units operated South Croydon to Milton Keynes services. They are dual voltage equipped for 25Kv ac overhead and 750V dc third rail. This facilitates a useful service from Bedford which provides passengers with interchange opportunities in London at several central locations including St Pancras International, City Thameslink and London Bridge. It also provides a direct service to Gatwick and Brighton. This clearly demonstrates a technical advance which the Class 4-CIG and 4-VEP units, which the Class 377 replaced, were never envisaged to require.

At Billingshurst we see a traditional, almost classic scene, with its station canopies and red brick station buildings and the adjacent Railway Inn meets the modern train design. Passengers on board will have little time to absorb such detail, as their train passes at quite some speed. The Class 377/4 is essentially the same as the Class 377/1, both of which have two Driving Motor Composite

Preston Park, Monday, 2 April 2012: Three Class 377/2 'Electrostar' EMUs, formed with First Capital Connect 377212 (based at Bedford Cauldwell Walk but carries previous SU Selhurst depot sticker) leading, and 377211 and 377207 in First Group 'Urban Lights' livery, pass with the 07.48 Bedford – Brighton.

158 • DIESEL AND ELECTRIC MOTIVE POWER ON THE SOUTHERN 1980s TO PRESENT

Billingshurst, Saturday, 26 June 2021: Southern Class 377/4 'Electrostar' 377432 passes with the 10.35 London Victoria to Southampton Central.

Pulborough, Tuesday, 3 April 2012: Southern Class 377/4 'Electrostar' 377432 arrives with the 14.26 service from London Victoria to Portsmouth and Southsea.

Open coaches, a Motor Standard Open and a Trailer Standard Open. The Class 377/4s were a later batch built in 2004-5 at Bombardier Transportation Derby.

This photograph shows the island platform for the Up line with the far left side no doubt previously serving the Midhurst branch trains. Pulborough station stands on the Three Bridges/Arundel railway line. It was first opened on 10 October 1859 and reached its maximum size and complexity in the first half of the twentieth century, with the completion of an island platform in December 1900, together with extensive sidings, a coal yard, cattle pens, a turntable, and goods shed.

The present Pulborough Signal Box, a Saxby & Farmer Type 5 design, was built in 1878. It was a widespread design and appeared on more than a dozen railways, including the London, Chatham & Dover Railway, the Great Eastern Railway and also in Ireland and overseas. It was particularly associated with the LB&SCR, where John Saxby had pioneered the use of mechanical interlocking of points and signals.

It's a fine early spring day in the picturesque beauty of the Arun valley in West Sussex, situated on the edge of the South Downs

Left and below: Monday, 2 April 2012, Arundel: Southern Class 377/1 or 377/4 'Electrostar' crosses over the water meadows near the River Arun and passes Arundel castle with a southbound early afternoon service from Horsham to Bognor Regis.

National Park. The prominent castle stands proud and embodies nearly a thousand years of history.

Passengers travelling along the nearby Sussex Coast route now benefit from the replacement of the increasingly unreliable Class 313s by Class 377 'Electrostars', which with their air-conditioning and accessible onboard toilets will certainly improve the travel experience of passengers on that route which incorporates Portsmouth to Brighton, Southsea, Bognor Regis to Littlehampton, Brighton to Lewes and Seaford.

The Class 377/5 was introduced into service from 2008/9 and supplied with dual voltage equipment for 25Kv ac overhead and 750V dc third rail. They were subleased by Southern to First Capital Connect and based at Bedford Cauldwell Walk . They operated Bedford to Three Bridges and Brighton services and later were transferred to Southeastern in 2016/17 when they were given their Southeastern blue livery and based at Selhurst depot.

Along with the Class 375 'Electrostar' fleet, the Class 377 fleet is also being given an upgrade under the 'Project Aurora' branding. The oldest of the Class 377s are estimated to have run over two million miles in service. It is funded by Porterbrook and is taking place over a four year period at a cost of £55 million. It will result in

Borough Green and Wrotham, Monday, 16 October 2023: Southeastern Class 377/5 'Electrostar' 377520 departs with the 11.31 London Charing Cross to Maidstone East (where trains were terminating due to engineering taking place on the line beyond there towards Ashford).

a fleet which will give improved operational performance through maintenance efficiency and extended life expectancy. Onboard data train recorders will facilitate diagnosis of faults, and passengers will benefit from new information and media screens. All seats are stripped out and rewiring for new plug points inserted.

Class 378 'Capitalstar'

Here's a narrative of London's Chelsea landmarks viewed from the Overground lines and the important link provided by the bridge for trains crossing the Thames to the west of the centre of London. In the second picture, the barge seen centre right appears to have raised the central section of its cover to reveal the interior of the barge ready to receive its new load.

The two chimneys are remnants of Lots Road Power Station. This was built in 1902 on Chelsea Creek and predates its limelight-hogging counterpart Battersea Power Station on the opposite side of the Thames by 39 years. It was commissioned by the Metropolitan District Electric Traction Company to provide power to the Metropolitan District Railway (now the District Line of the London Underground railway network). Two new glass residential

Balcombe, Monday, 2 April 2012: First Capital Connect Class 377/5 'Electrostar' 377508 passes with an early afternoon service from Bedford to Brighton.

London, Chelsea Railway Bridge, Friday, 11 May 2012: First picture: A London Overground 'Capitalstar' Class 378 crosses the River Thames with a mid-afternoon service from Stratford via West Hampstead to Clapham Junction via the North London line. Second picture: A London Overground 'Capitalstar' Class 378 crosses the River Thames with a mid-afternoon service via West Hampstead to Stratford via the North London line.

SECOND GENERATION ELECTRIC MULTIPLE UNITS • 163

towers which frame the power station have been constructed at the mouth of the creek .To preserve the historic structure and its remaining two chimneys (two were taken down when it was closed), a new apartment complex, opened late September 2022, has been built inside the original skin.

These Class 378 'Capitalstar' trains were new to service in July 2009 and still look new to service as seen here a year later. Such Class 378/1 units are equipped only for 750V dc third rail. Their cab design looks smart and neat, tidy and more rounded when compared to the sharp, blunt lines of previous modern designs. The train interiors carry longitudinal seating facilitating high capacity provision for standing passengers and easier movement within the train, so avoiding the traditional crowding around door exits. Fine wrought- iron canopy brackets contribute to the station's metropolitan atmosphere. The Overground's interconnections with many routes enhance its potential for journeys from west to east that are possible using its orbital network which navigates third rail and overhead power supplies and serves as an important freight route, most significantly between Willesden and Stratford. It shares

Richmond, Saturday, 5 June 2010: Class 378 'Capitalstar' EMUs 013 and 017 await duties in providing services on the North London line section of the London Overground system. A District line train awaits passengers at the far right.

tracks with London Underground's trains between Richmond and Gunnersbury. The Class 378 'Capitalstar' EMUs are constantly busy throughout the day with passengers travelling short and longer distances without having to change trains or navigate the congested Underground.

Class 387 'Electrostar'

Here's an eye-catching livery featuring the Gatwick Express motif. Twenty-seven of these 4-car units were ordered by Govia Thameslink Railway and delivered in 2016. They include more generous luggage space as compared to the earlier Class 387/1s now used on GWR London Paddington to Reading and Didcot services. They replaced the Gatwick Express Class 460 'Juniper' 8-car EMUs previously used on the Gatwick Express services, which looked rather like something from a James Bond film set with their distinctive, sloping cab fronts.

The Class 387/2s are capable of 110mph and are equipped with air-conditioning. Alongside the high-profile Gatwick Express services, they are also used to provide a number of fast and semi-fast services between London Victoria and Brighton.

Gatwick Airport, Thursday, 27 September 2018: A pair of Southern Class 387/2 'Electrostar' EMUs, with 387205 at the rear, departs with an afternoon service to London Victoria.

Class 395 'Javelin'

The Class 395 'Javelin' units are routed via HS1 (High Speed 1) from London St Pancras to Ashford, thereafter closely following alongside the conventional Network Rail line to Folkestone before joining the coastal route to Dover and Ramsgate. Operated by Southeastern, they all stop at Ashford. Ordered in 2004, they are formed of six cars, with two unpowered driving cars (each carrying a pantograph) and four powered vehicles. They are technically advanced, bearing a design used by Hitachi for their A-train family and 400-Series Shinkansen trains in Japan, equipped for various signalling systems and different power supplies. Their ability to accelerate quickly and maintain a speed of 140mph means that they can comfortably fit in to schedules shared with Eurostar services on the HS1. They have proved highly reliable in service and this has significantly contributed to their customer appeal and attraction to the wider public. Such is justified, for they provide a journey time to and from London St Pancras that is nearly half that taken by the conventional (third-rail) route to London Victoria or Charing Cross.

Construction of HS1 (completed in three separate stages) finally made it possible to provide domestic high-speed services from

Dover, Saturday, 14 October 2023: A Class 395 'Javelin' approaches the Port of Dover with the 12.04 St Pancras International to Ramsgate.

a substantial area of Kent to St Pancras after the very slow and meandering route into Waterloo used initially by the Eurostars was replaced by the high speed route direct from St Pancras to the Channel Tunnel. The full high speed service started in 2009. Travel time for the fastest services is just one hour and three minutes.

Ramsgate in steam days was the terminus of the *Thanet Belle* which operated from May 1948, when it was in the hands of Bulleid Light Pacifics which were based at Ramsgate and at Stewarts Lane. Its name was later changed to the *Kentish Belle* to celebrate the 1951 'Festival of Britain'. By the mid-1950s, 'King Arthur' class 4-6-0s were often provided for this service. Maunsell 'N' class Moguls were at this time used on less prestigious services to Ramsgate.

The steam shed here was closed in 1959 once third rail electrification had reached the Kent coast. Unusually, the steam shed was rebuilt and extended as an EMU depot operating alongside a former carriage shed, which was similarly adapted. The depot is adjacent to Ramsgate station and acts as the home of Southeastern's Class 375 fleet, and a new building was constructed in 2009 to service the high-speed Class 395 Javelins. Their design appearance presents a business-like image and their livery befits their purpose as providing speed and reliability. Sunday afternoons are certainly busy with those who have travelled to the coast for

Ramsgate, Saturday, 14 October 2023: Class 395 'Javelin' units with right, 395020 having arrived with the 13.37 from St Pancras International, and left, 395013 having arrived with the 13.07 from St Pancras International.

the weekend making their return journey to the Capital. Saturday afternoons, as here, are much quieter – when those who wish to spend time at the coast can enjoy a decent length of visit thanks to the short journey time from and to St Pancras.

Here we see the Class 395 'Javelin' demonstrating use of its dual-voltage equipment along the HS1 section of its journey under the wires as far as Ashford, from where it proceeds drawing power from the third rail, travelling at a more sedentary pace towards Ramsgate via Folkestone and Dover, as contrasted with the route taken by the 12.37 service from St Pancras International which reaches Ramsgate via Canterbury West and goes forward to Margate and Faversham.

The twenty-nine strong fleet of Class 395 Javelins, built by Hitachi between 2007 and 2009, powered by four Hitachi asynchronous traction motors of 210kW capable of 140mph, is at the time of writing undergoing an interior upgrade and refresh at Ashford Depot, where they have been serviced and maintained at their purpose-built facility. There is a team-based approach adopted with the Class 395 fleet's maintenance, which is assisted by the engineering, maintenance and procurement personnel working together in the same office, which promotes the efficient sharing of information to solve problems as they arise. Interestingly there are

Boxley, Monday, 16 October 2023: A Class 395 'Javelin' passes at speed forming the 13.07 St Pancras International to Ramsgate.

no third rails or overhead power lines within the maintenance shed; power is supplied via heavy-duty cables attached to the trains' third rail shoes which provides adequate power to move the train to a safe distance outside the shed where the train can reconnect to the third rail supply. The refresh and upgrade sees the fleet receiving new carpeting and seats, USB charging points at seat, LED lighting and a live passenger information system upgrade with new media screens.

Class 442 Wessex Express and Gatwick Express

With the route from Bournemouth to Weymouth electrified in 1988, this fleet of twenty-four units replaced the need for a Class 432 4-REP (Restaurant EPB) unit to be detached from Waterloo to Weymouth trains at Bournemouth in order for a Class 33 to be attached to work the remaining 4-TC set forward. This operation added time and cost to running the through Weymouth services. These new Express units were permitted to run at 100mph over some sections of the South Western main line west of Pirbright Junction. They were also diagrammed for services from London Waterloo to Portsmouth from 1992. Their formation included a Motor Buffet Luggage Standard (MBLS) which incorporated a buffet area with a small area of seating, the Guard's compartment and two luggage compartments. Later the Parcels Sector re-evaluated the requirement for the room required for the parcels on these sets and

Woking, Saturday, 28 May 1988: centre left: Class 423 4-VEP 3045 with the 11.12 to Aldershot, 10.36 from London Waterloo; right: Class 442 'Wessex Express' units 2403 and 2409 form the 10.45 ex-London Waterloo, 11.11 Woking to Poole.

thus released one of the two luggage compartments which were converted to a lounge area attached to the buffet.

Enthusiasts and the general public welcomed the aesthetic look of the cab on these Class 442 'Wessex Express' EMUs, which in part recalled the 'Clacton Express' Class 309s to which they bore quite a resemblance, and was considered less austere than the cabs provided for contemporary Class 317 and 455 units.

They were equipped with four English Electric traction motors type EE546 of 300kW, previously used in the Class 432 4-REPs, and were refurbished at Chart Leacon prior to their move to Derby Works for fitting into the new carriages, thus echoing the Southern Region's tendency to reuse and recycle equipment . However, the bodywork was entirely of a new design and based on Mk.3b stock. This brought 23m length vehicles to the Southern for the first time. It permitted the previous use of 12-car EMU formations to be replaced by two 5-car units. Their consist was of a DTC and a Driving Trailer Standard along with, in between these, two Trailer Standards and an MBLS. They are fitted with brake hoses and train-supply cables for occasions when towed by a locomotive over non-electrified lines.

In 2008, Southern acquired the franchise for services to Gatwick Airport, merging such with their services to Brighton. They were allocated some of the 442s for this service commencing in the late autumn of 2008, carrying a distinct Gatwick Express livery. As they

Eastleigh, Saturday,
16 October 1999: Class 442 'Wessex Express' 2423 in South West Trains livery passes with the 11.30 London Waterloo to Weymouth.

First picture: Gatwick Airport, Friday, 29 May 2009: Southern Trains 'Gatwick Express' Class 442 442404 in freshly painted Gatwick Express livery departs with the 13.20 to London Victoria. Second picture: Preston Park, Monday, 2 April 2012: A pair of Class 442 'Gatwick Express' units, with 442407 at the rear, pass with a mid-morning service for Gatwick Airport and London Victoria.

were transferred to Southern for integration with timetabled trains from Victoria to Brighton, so the 'Juniper' Alstom Class 460s which had operated the Gatwick Express services were withdrawn.

From February 2016, new Class 387/2 'Electrostars' were introduced to service along the Victoria to Brighton line, leaving just a few Class 442s providing peak-hour enhancement diagrams.

March 2017 saw the last few units withdrawn from service. Following significant refurbishment and reallocation to London to Portsmouth services, the Class 442s made a limited reappearance, although several safety issues arose which saw the Class fleet withdrawn in September 2019. Attempts to rectify these faults were thwarted by Covid, and their last dates in service were in March 2020.

Class 444 Desiro

Siemens maintained a design and construction base in Düsseldorf, which facilitated the adaptation of its electric unit designs to the UK market where imminent replacement of slam door stock on the Southern would be requisite in the first part of the new millennium. Their 'Desiro' product was already available in mainland Europe. Renewed award of the London and South West franchise to South West Trains, owned by Stagecoach, incorporated a commitment to replace the slam door stock and 'Desiro' electric units formed an essential part of this revolutionary plan, with construction of the Class 444 and 450 for outer suburban and main line longer-distance services

This attractive station, at New Milton, was built in 1886 for the Brockenhurst to Christchurch Branch Railway, opened to traffic in 1888. The location was advertised, along with Barton-on-Sea and

London Waterloo, Saturday, 14 May 2005: Class 444 'Desiro' 5-car EMUs operated by South West Trains, with left, 444024 stabled awaiting its scheduled diagram; and right, 444030 forming the 13.09 to Portsmouth Harbour.

Saturday, 8 August 2009, New Milton: South West Trains Class 444 'Desiro' 444015 arrives with the 15.05 London Waterloo to Weymouth.

Milford-on-Sea, in railway posters endeavouring to attract visitors to sample the delights of this area 'Twixt New Forest and Sea'.

The fleet of forty-five Class 444 'Desiro' units were built at the Siemens factory in Vienna and tested at the Wildenrath test circuit. Introduced from 2003-05, they were primarily built to replace the Class 442 'Wessex Express' electric units as well as any remaining slam door stock used on the London Waterloo to Southampton, Poole and Weymouth services. The 5-car units are formed of two driving power cars and two intermediate Trailer Standard Opens (TSO), along with a modified TSO which incorporates a guard's office and a small buffet/shop counter. They are equipped with a passenger information system, and single leaf sliding plug doors. Seating is in open saloons 2+1 facing and unidirectional in first class. The trains are capable of 100mph.

These trains are used on the London Waterloo to Southampton, Poole and Weymouth main line along with services from Waterloo to Portsmouth via Guildford and Eastleigh. They can work in multiple with sister Class 450 as well as Class 444 units. Each unit provides 327 Standard Class seats and 32 First Class seats. They facilitate disabled access and feature large external door operation buttons, with explanation of the operation of the button supplied in English and Braille. A chime sounds when the doors have been activated and an alarm sounds when they are closing.

The Class 444s are currently operated by South Western Railway which took over the South Western franchise from South West Trains in August 2017 after rail operators First Group and Hong Kong-based Mass Transit Railway (MTR) won the contract and rebranded their new acquisition as South Western Railway. There is debate about whether the South Western Railway livery featured in this photograph is any improvement on that of South West Trains. A bright blue, grid-like symbol is incorporated within the logo and appears along with a condensed version of the logo seen on the new livery that uses the acronym 'SWR'.

Seen climbing the 1 in 50 gradient on Upwey Bank, see page 174, close to the site of Upwey Wishing Well halt that would on Summer Saturdays in steam days have featured pilot locomotives (frequently 'N' Class Moguls, Standard tanks or even rebuilt 'West Country' locomotives) providing assistance to lengthy passenger trains as far as Dorchester. As for these Class 444s, they effortlessly glide up the Bank! They certainly had to earn public support for their replacement of the previous high standards of comfort and reliability set by the Class 442s. As for the traditional livery of Stagecoach white and bright blue, yellow and red seen worn by

Bincombe Tunnel (south portal), Saturday, 6 August 2022: South Western Railway Class 444 'Desiro' 444020 is about to enter the tunnel mouth with the 12.20 semi-fast service to London Waterloo from Weymouth.

Right and below: Upwey Bank, Saturday, 6 August 2022: first picture, South Western Railway Class 444 'Desiro' 444034 ascends the climb out of Weymouth (with the Isle of Portland in the background) forming the 16.20 semi-fast Weymouth to London Waterloo; second picture, South Western Railway Class 444 'Desiro' 444021 with the 16.03 fast service from Weymouth to London Waterloo.

Weymouth, Saturday, 6 August 2022: South Western Railway Class 444 'Desiro' 444005 stabled at platform.

444034, or the newer South Western Railway livery worn by 444021, I leave the reader to select their preference.

In a traditional, time-honoured method of operation, pairs of Class 444 work as far as Bournemouth from London Waterloo with one set detached there whilst the remaining set goes forward to Poole and Weymouth. This partly recalls the separation of 4-TC stock from the 4-REPs at Bournemouth and the Class 33s taking charge of the 4-TCs to Weymouth. On Summer Saturdays in the early 1980s, through boat-train services to Weymouth Quay delivered passengers to and collected passengers from the Channel Islands liners. Regular services to the Quay ended shortly after 1987, although a number of special trains were permitted down the route in the 1990s. Removal of the rails along the Quay has deemed any future use by trains out of the question.

Class 450 Desiro

Like the Class 444 'Desiro' units, these were built at the Siemens factory in Vienna and tested at the Wildenrath test circuit. Introduced from 2002-07 and powered by the same four Siemens 1TB2016 250 kW traction motors as the Class 444, the first of the Class to be delivered to the UK was 450007 which arrived at Bournemouth depot in December 2002. However, before these trains could be

Clapham Junction, Saturday, 14 May 2005: A pair of Class 450 'Desiro' outer-suburban 4-car EMUs with 450034 leading, in South West Trains outer-suburban livery, operating a west-bound early afternoon service for Staines and Windsor and Eton Riverside.

introduced to service, upgrades to the third rail power supply and extensive testing along with extensive driver training would be required. Such testing initially took place overnight between Dorchester and Weymouth during February 2003. A £1.5 million driver training centre was constructed at Basingstoke, incorporating some of the most advanced interactive simulators to assist real life operations and scenarios. A significant re-training programme for drivers formed an essential part of the potential realisation to introduce these new trains into service.

Exactly a year later on this date, this service was formed of two Class 458 'Junipers', which just goes to show that a photograph can become history in a comparatively short time! In the new millennium, fleets serving the Southern are representative of the suburban trains in service on the Continent, where new train fleets are built by well established firms including Siemens and Bombardier, or by Alsthom for France's railways and in the case of Switzerland, Stadler's articulated Fast Light Intercity and Regional Train electric units or Hitachi Rail Italy's various offerings. The train product and maintenance package now come together as part of the purchase contract, thus facilitating the provision of technical supplies over lengthy periods of time.

SECOND GENERATION ELECTRIC MULTIPLE UNITS • 177

Chiswick, Saturday, 11 March 2023: A pair of Class 450 'Desiro' outer-suburban 4-car EMUs with 450040 leading, in South Western Railway livery, approaches with the 10.03 Weybridge to London Waterloo.

Clapham Junction, Wednesday, 5 July 2023: Class 450 'Desiro' outer-suburban 4-car EMUs with 450065, in South Western Railway livery, leading no less than two more Class 450s with a mid-afternoon service from London Waterloo to Alton.

Seen below Clapham Junction's impressive footbridge, the length of this train suggests that it has already been strengthened for the late afternoon rush hour, or it may have kept this formation throughout the day – so avoiding the logistics of part of the train running ecs post-morning rush hour to storage sidings at Wimbledon depot – or beyond – and finding paths to and from that location back to Waterloo. Multiply that infinitely for London Waterloo's late afternoon rush hour, and you start to see complexities necessary for deploying ecs trains ready for the rush hour.

Class 455

The disused platforms tell their own story, recalling the busy days of steam-hauled specials and vintage electric units such as 3-SUBs on race days when all the platforms would have seen use. The branch from Sutton was electrified by 17 June 1928. Pullman, first class and Lord Derby's specials continued to use Epson Downs until 1939 and, with the exception of the latter, resumed until 1953.

Following on from the Class 210 DEMUs which were built as prototypes by BREL and entered service in 1982, and which spent most of their careers based at Reading depot, it was decided to construct an all-steel integrally constructed suburban unit with carriages which were essentially a shortened form of the standard Mk 3 InterCity carriage design. Traction was supplied by four GEC/Brush type 507 traction motors providing 1,000hp. In typical Southern tradition, the motor bogies had reconditioned traction motors, recovered from withdrawn 4-SUB and 2-HAP units, and were therefore limited to 75mph. They replaced the 4-SUBs after

Epsom Downs, Saturday, 22 November 1986: Class 455 5804 awaits departure with the 15.21 to London Victoria.

SECOND GENERATION ELECTRIC MULTIPLE UNITS • 179

delivery started in 1983. The redesigned front that was eventually applied to the Class 455/7 units, introduced 1984, looked much better, with a streamlined roof profile and with the raised box in the cab roof eliminated, although the cab front was still cluttered by jumper cables. The latter sub-class included a non driving trailer from the former Class 508 units, which rendered such units distinctive being from an entirely different profile and design developed for use in the Mersey tunnels!

Class 456

Another Class to share the Mk 3 InterCity carriage profile with the Class 455 was the BREL constructed 2-car Class 456, introduced to service in September 1991. Prominent in the cab-front appearance are the coupling pipes for use when working in multiple with other sets of the same Class. They were powered by two English Electric 507 traction motors and top speed was 75mph which would have suited their use on inner suburban services with short distances between stations such as those on the South London line served by this train. Although initially delivered to the South Western Division, South Central Division's need for new trains meant that all twenty-four of the Class 456 were transferred to their train fleet, which permitted the withdrawal of the 2-HAP units and for the transfer of most of the remaining 2-EPB units to Slade Green on the

Clapham Junction, Tuesday, 26 May 2009: Southern Class 456 456020 forms a southbound early afternoon service, very possibly the 13.49 London Victoria to London Bridge. On the right is First GB Railfreight Class 66/7 66715 hauling a southbound Metronet engineering train.

South Eastern Division, where the Class 465 and 466 'Networker' fleet would replace them. The Class 456 were equipped to work with Class 455. The Class 456 fleet was finally withdrawn from service in March 2022.

Class 458 Juniper

This train is seen using the former Eurostar International Terminal and is viewed under the impressively restored asymmetric roof. Various sizes of sheets of glass are placed in an overlapping configuration that can flex and expand in respond to the roof's various twists and turns. It was an ingenious and meticulous design and admired as one of the most iconic roof structures of that era with distinctive blue steel work adding further refinement. The long arched and curved terminus building only served its intended purpose for thirteen years, from its opening in 1994 to closure in 2007. Eventually St Pancras International would shift passengers bound for the European continent away from Waterloo once HS1 was constructed. The station terminal was then closed and mothballed for over a decade.

The former terminal was eventually refurbished by AECOM Architects which provided renovated platforms, concourse space and retail premises to the station. The former 'Eurostar' platforms

London Waterloo, Saturday, 11 March 2023: South Western Railway Class 458/5 458523 accompanied by a second unit has arrived with a mid-morning service.

20-24 were brought back into service in May 2019 after partial re-opening in December 2018. They now accommodate nearly all the Reading/Bracknell line services.

Trains from the Reading via Bracknell route would have usually terminated at Waterloo's platforms 18 and 19 prior to the re-opening of the former Eurostar International Terminal referred to above. This train is most likely to have come from that route as it is on one of the far side Down lines.

The fleet of thirty 'Juniper Coradia' Class 458 EMUs, now formed of five cars though initially introduced as four cars, and built by Alstom GEC, were until relatively recently route-dedicated to the services from London Waterloo to Windsor Riverside, Hounslow via Brentford and via Richmond, Weybridge and Reading. They replaced the 4-VEP and 4-CIG slam door units previously used on these routes until their introduction to service in February 2000. Between 2013 and 2016, this fleet of 4-car units and the former Gatwick Express fleet of eight 8-car Class 460 units was combined to form a fleet of thirty-six 5-car Standard Class only 458/5s.

Although the first unit was completed in October 1998, there was a slow start to their introduction, the final unit being introduced in October 2002. There remained issues with the design and performance of these trains such as issues with the end gangway's

Clapham Junction, Thursday, 27 September 2018: South Western Railway Class 458/5 458508 passes en route to London Waterloo.

London Cannon Street, Friday, 15 January 2016: A Southeastern Class 465 awaits morning departure for its North Kent destination amidst the remaining towers of Cannon Street's original station and Wren's Neoclassic, Gothic and Baroque influenced masterpiece of St Paul's Cathedral.

design favouring semi-permanent formations of trains rather than the Southern tradition of coupling and uncoupling trains to fit intensity of passenger use. Once a train had been coupled or uncoupled, onboard computers then had to be rebooted – a problem experienced with numerous new fleets in later years. The Class 485 was finally withdrawn from service in May 2022.

Class 465 Networker

Built from 1991-94, these electric units are now somewhat elderly unsung citizens coming from the 'Network 2000' rolling stock renewal in which Network SouthEast had a substantial role. The underlying reason for this was the need to replace the traditional slam door stock which was characterised by the 2-EPB and 4-EPB units which first saw service in the 1950s. Commuter travel into London was steadily increasing, and the impact of Network SouthEast in raising the profile of quality and pride in the south east's rails was certainly encouraging such.

In order to replace the slam door stock including the 4-VEPs, new 4-car electric units were built to serve the Kent Coast diagrams and south eastern division commuter lines. These would be nominated 'Class 465' and branded as 'Kent Link Networker'. Construction of their aluminium body shells (to help reduce weight over an equivalent train built of steel) was carried out at BREL York and at Metro-Cammell. They were fitted with buffers – an advantage over the Class 465s. Formation was of Driving Motor Standard Opens each end of two Trailer Standard Opens and power was provided by Hitachi or GEC-Alsthom traction motors providing 280kW. Seating was a little on the cramped side, but suitable for generally short distance commuter journeys.

Covering the twenty-one mile distance in nearly an hour, stopping services from Sevenoaks serve

SECOND GENERATION ELECTRIC MULTIPLE UNITS • **183**

either Charing Cross or Blackfriars. Faster services from Hastings or Ramsgate are likely choices for most passengers heading into the City. The livery of overall white with black window surrounds and light blue doors with, on some units, a dark blue lower bodyside stripe, appeals when kept clean! Class 465/9 is the sub-Class for those units given a refurbish in 2005 for longer distance journeys.

Sevenoaks, Saturday, 14 October 2023: Southeastern Class 465 465908 departs with the 10.01 for London Charing Cross.

Class 700 Desiro City

This fleet of sixty 8-car and fifty-five 12-car, dual voltage units built by Siemens and equipped for drawing power from 750V dc third rail and 25kV ac overhead, proved particularly unpopular when first introduced into service between 2016 and 2018, with their spartan metallic interiors and low density hard seating hardly matching the comfort of the Class 387/2 'Electrostar' units used on the Gatwick Express. After all, they were intended for long distance journeys in cases of passengers potentially travelling through to Bedford, Cambridge or Peterborough from Brighton and stations on the Brighton main line. They did however facilitate such

Gatwick Airport, Thursday, 27 September 2018: Thameslink Class 700 'Desiro City' 700116 approaches with a mid-afternoon service.

journeys without having to change trains or undertake travel to other London termini for onward journeys. The Class was designed with modular component technology including remote diagnostics which reduced maintenance times and facilitated replacement parts when needed. They were supplied with several safety systems including ERTMS (European Rail Traffic Management System) and Automatic Train Operation which would be requisite for the tunnel sections through London with a potential capacity of up to twenty-four trains per hour in each direction.

The regenerative braking capability of these units means that they are up to fifty per cent more energy efficient than the Class 319s that they replaced. The intensity of service through the tunnels is enhanced by their dual voltage capability, and facilitates the metro-style service which sees them using a two-track section under central London which demands a high level of reliability and performance from this train fleet. Their spartan functional interior provides a light and airy saloon with large doors and windows, and open gangways to facilitate passenger movement throughout the train. Their maintenance base is at the relatively new Three Bridges Traincare facility at Crawley.

SECOND GENERATION ELECTRIC MULTIPLE UNITS • **185**

Sevenoaks, Friday, 13 October: Thameslink Class 700 'Desiro City' 700002 awaits departure with the 12.52 service to London Blackfriars via Bat & Ball and Otford.

Class 701 Aventra

These trains have suffered significant delays to their introduction to inner and outer suburban service on South Western lines, including the Bracknell/Reading route, which should have taken place during 2021–22 and yet the pictures on page 186 show their storage awaiting test-mileage accumulation and driver training in mid-July 2023, with units entering service in March 2024 on the Windsor & Eton line. Their first passenger-carrying duty was actually on 9 January 2024, which was kept as low key as possible. They were late in delivery as a result of issues with their construction by Bombardier and by software issues including that of the train control and management system (TCMS) which has proved particularly complex.

There are two versions of the train formations with sixty 10-car Class 701/0 and thirty 5-car Class 701/5. They are promised to provide greater seating capacity, improved performance, wider and faster opening doors, provision of cycle racks, and charging points at every seat. Regenerative braking will assist in efficient energy usage.

The branding 'Arterio' is supposed to recall the artery of branch lines and main lines forming an intricate network of suburban lines

Right and below: Clapham Junction, Wednesday, 5 July 2023; in the first picture is a South Western Railway Class 450 'Desiro' outer-suburban 4-car EMU '450011' passing with a mid-afternoon service to London Waterloo while, to the right, are seen stabled South Western Railway Class 701 'Aventra' units 701037 and 701014. In the second picture Class 701 'Aventra' units 701017 and 701028 are seen stabled alongside Class 450 450034 'Desiro' EMU.

served by South Western Railway. With such a late delivery of these new trains – over four years – it begs the question 'What happens if the artery ceases to function properly?' The Train Drivers' Union ASLEF even declared the 'Aventras' as 'unfit for purpose' because of the complex difficulties with the TCMS and many other significant teething problems. During their first months in service there was a recognised need to undertake a 'whole suite of modifications and upgrades required as we go along' according to the South Western Railway Engineering Director. A long list of remedies required for addressing has included problems with door obstacle detection technology, cab design, and the coupling and uncoupling process (as occurred with the Class 458s).

Here is one of the 10-car sets in service looking very smart and new in its company livery. The trains are popular on this route with visiting tourists to London for there is, of course, Windsor castle to see and you can enjoy a quick language lesson by listening to their conversations on board, and consequently the lengthy train is easily justified.

The District line from Wimbledon to destinations of Edgware Road or South Kensington onwards adds an extra attraction here as it crosses the Waterloo to Reading main line which threads through a deep cutting close to Putney. Indeed, it will soon cross the Thames and visitors to Putney can enjoy a journey to the City via National Rail, TfL Underground or by Uber boat operated by Thames Clippers (which operate from this western limit to Barking Riverside or any of the twenty piers en route).

Putney, Thursday, 25 April 2024: South Western Railway Class 701 'Aventra' unit 701043 approaches the station with the 11.33 London Waterloo to Windsor and Eton Riverside.

Class 707 Desiro City

This fleet of thirty 5-car units is an extension of the order for Class 700 Siemens 'Desiro City' trains built at the same time (for different operators) although these draw power only from the third rail (and are wired for overhead 25kV ac). Ordered in 2014, they entered service during August 2017 along routes to Weybridge via Virginia Water, Staines, and Windsor. They were also introduced to service

Clapham Junction, Thursday, 27 September 2018: South Western Railway Class 707 'Desiro City' 707021 passes en route to London Waterloo mid-afternoon with a service probably from Windsor Riverside.

on the outer suburban lines. However, their introduction coincided with the change of franchise from South West Trains to South Western Railway, operated by First and MTR. This caused a very significant change consequent to the new management preferring to replace them with the Class 701s. It seems incredible that the new Class 707 trains were to be replaced by yet another fleet of new trains, albeit of a different design. Photographs of the Class 707s in service quickly became history. Consequent to the much delayed Class 701s being introduced to traffic, the removal of the Class 707s meant, to the detriment of passengers on the routes mentioned, that their diagrams needed to be operated by older Class 455s and somewhat newer Class 444 and 458 trains, with a lower quality of train interior and facilities. As result of the sustained delay to the introduction of the Class 701s, South Western Railway retained 12 Class 707 EMUs into 2022 to support adequate capacity.

SECOND GENERATION ELECTRIC MULTIPLE UNITS • 189

Southeastern grabbed the unexpected bonus of this now - spare brand new fleet of trains to help replace their elderly 'Networkers' as well as some of the 'Electrostars' and at the same time to improve the quality of train provided on the more inner suburban services that they provide. Transfers took place in January 2021, and these Class 707s were nominated for the franchise's new City Beam services, mostly working out of London Charing Cross and Cannon Street to Sevenoaks or Dartford and Gravesend from September 2021. Some Class 707s remained with South Western Railway to supply the need for adequate trains to cover their routes during the Class 701 debacle until September 2023. The 'City Beam' route map showing, in lime green, the routes covered by these Class 707s is clear to read with other parts of their network in Kent also shown in Southeastern blue hue.

Sevenoaks, Friday, 13 October 2023: Southeastern Class 707 'Desiro City' 707008 with *City Beam* branding departs on the 12.36 to London Charing Cross.

PART 7

Eurostar

Class 373 Eurostar

These train sets were introduced for the ground-breaking services under the Channel in November 1994. SNCF owned several 'Eurostar' units for use on internal services from Paris Nord to Lille. These were not permitted to operate through the Channel Tunnel. In Britain, seven 8-car sets were built for Regional 'Eurostar' services which would have started in May 1997. These would form direct services from Manchester to Paris/Brussels, Birmingham to Paris and Glasgow to Paris/Brussels. In comparison to the 20-car sets (including power cars) of coupled 10-car sets which formed the Waterloo to Paris/Brussels services, the regional services would be formed of pairs of 8-car sets (including power cars). A financial review of the proposed services saw the scheme cancelled, especially

Paddock Wood, Friday, 31 October 1997: A Class 373 'Eurostar' passes with the 12.19 Paris Nord to London Waterloo.

in view of passenger numbers using 'Eurostar' services being much lower than forecast.

The eight Class 373s retained by Eurostar are being fitted with Hitachi Bi-Standard in-cab signalling which combines Transmission Voie Machine, already used on trains using the Channel Tunnel HS1 route and on high-speed lines in France, with ERTMS which will permit them to use other cross-border high speed routes than those already used. Eurostar Class 374 Siemens Velaro e320s are already equipped with the latter.

Ashford International is no longer served by Eurostar which severely cut back its services during and after the pandemic. Eurostar is currently focusing on its most profitable inter-capital routes. The 'Brexit' factor also contributes problems. British passports have to be stamped in and out and because 40 per cent of Eurostar passengers are British, this adds considerably to the processing time at stations. Consequently, the UK border force has to prioritise St Pancras rather than divert resources to Ebbsfleet or Ashford which have therefore at least for the present been omitted from station calls. Eventually, Eurostar aims to relaunch extended services to Bourg-Saint Maurice, Marseille or Disneyland Paris, although they prefer to enhance the potential of open hubs such as Lille Europe and Brussels Midi.

Boxley, Monday, 16 October 2023: A class 373 'Eurostar' passes at speed with the 13.01 service from St Pancras International to Brussels Midi.

Finale

**Brighton, Wednesday, 23 June 2021
Volk's Electric Railway:** Car 6.

It would be inexcusable to omit reference to this heritage electric railway on which many tourists arriving at Brighton's Southern terminus would no doubt have enjoyed the mile long journey alongside the promenade and literally hugging the beach. Fortunately, this unique railway has recently received significant restoration and remains a popular visitor attraction, winning the prestigious award of 'Railway of the Year' for 2023.

A product of Magnus Volk, a Brighton designer, this then-2ft gauge railway, electrified at 110V dc, opened in 1883. April 1884 saw a rebuild at a revised gauge of 2ft 9in. It was soon converted to an off-centre three rail system owing to serious leakages of current when sea water washed over the line. At around the same time, the gauge was again altered to 2ft 8.5in. A large raised 'Electric railway' sign adorned the entrance at Aquarium station. Photographs of packed pairs of tram cars show that the railway was very popular. The railway in modern times has enjoyed the benefits of a successful Heritage Lottery application in 2015 funding a new building and visitor centre. After substantial upgrade work on the line, it was reopened in full between Aquarium and Black Rock in May 2022.

Car 6 was originally a 32-seater and entered service in 1901. It is understood to have started out as a cross bench open but by 1924 it had been converted to a standard semi-open with sliding doors. These semi-opens' survival for over a century and well into the current decade is a tribute to their practical and robust design.

Folkestone Junction station was opened in 1843 and later was renamed Folkestone East, closed in 1965. The short 1,328yd Folkestone Harbour branch served the Harbour at 111ft below the main line. In steam days, the exceptional gradients of 1 in 30/36 required four tank engines to push and pull trains up the gradient – the weight restriction on the swing bridge at the harbour meant heavier locomotives were banned. The luxurious VSOE carriages recall the *Brighton Belle* Pullman EMUs. After its withdrawal during the Second World War years, this famed train was reinstated in October 1946 and by the 1960s there were four such trains each way between London and Brighton. The South Eastern and Chatham Railway ordered twelve dedicated Pullman carriages – six Parlour First and six Kitchen Firsts – to be constructed for use in the *Orient Express*. Six were constructed by the Birmingham Carriage and Wagon Company, and six at the Pullman Car Company, These entered service on London to Dover boat trains between October 1920 and January 1921.Some of these prestigious carriages survived the war and then found their use in the *Bournemouth Belle*.

Folkestone East, Sunday, 24 August 1986: VSOE stock is seen en route to Folkestone Harbour, awaiting its Class 33 train locomotive 33027 to run around. On the right, 4-CEP units are stabled in the carriage sidings.

Maybe the passengers on board the VSOE seen above would, in its 1930s heyday, have been persuaded to visit the continent after seeing the colourful and interesting poster jointly issued by the GWR, LMS, LNER and Southern railways which portrays a picture by W. Smithson Broadhead and now owned by the National Railway Museum. It is entitled *The Continent* and features a 1930s Parisian cafeteria scene in which two immaculately dressed and flirtatious couples are clearly enjoying a dalliance in Paris!

The Southern epitomised the rural branch line, through London's leafy outer-suburbs, the Kentish Weald, the Winchelsea Marshes, the coastal splendours of the Isle of Wight, the Cretaceous chalk slopes of the North and South Downs, the splendour of Dorset's seaside towns or the now-closed branches to several of East Devon's coastal resorts. The fact that its tentacles extended to Okehampton, Padstow, and Ilfracombe meant that it actually ventured far in to the West Country. The enchanting countryside to the north of Dartmoor was purely Southern and the remaining lengthy Barnstaple branch

Yeoford, Monday, 14 November 2022: Class 158/9 158957 departs with the 11.35 Barnstaple to Exeter Central.

retains a traditional unspoilt character. Train fleets along this line have undergone many changes, from locomotive hauled trains to the unwelcome Pacers and Sprinters which are now replaced by more comfortable Class 158 and 166 DMUs.

Here's another line exuding Southern atmosphere in modern times with characterful Kentish stations such as Chislehurst which sees fast and semi-fast services passing through on the Kent main line as well as stopping trains to more local retreats. Here the station appears deserted during the early afternoon. The freshened-up platform canopies and lattice girders, tasteful colour scheme on the wrought iron pillars and clean station brickwork helps convey a sense of heritage and atmosphere through which the rather ubiquitous modular style conveyed by the passing electric units reminds of the purpose that these architectural features serve.

It's always interesting to see the various retro-liveries applied to modern fleets in their final days recalling their times in BR or early privatisation, such as those seen applied to the CrossCountry and GWR HSTs and the Class 507 EMU on Merseyrail during their final weeks of service. It offers a form of tribute to trains which

Chislehurst, Saturday, 11 March 2023: Southeastern Class 375/6 'Electrostar' 375628 passes with the 12.59 London Charing Cross to Dover Priory.

Putney, Thursday, 25 April 2024: South Western Railway Class 455/8 455868 leads Class 455/9 455906 as it departs with the 10.27 London Waterloo to London Waterloo via Kingston.

have remained in service far longer than planned. Certainly the interesting fleet hosted by Locomotive Services pays tribute to a variety of previous liveries worn relevant to the locomotives when in service. How well that BR blue and grey now looks when it is not simply one of thousands of trains given the same 'blue' colours!

Bibliography

BackTrack Volume 8 No.5, September/October 1994
BackTrack Volume 10 No.2, February 1996
BackTrack Volume 10 No.3, March 1996
BR Gradient Main Line Profiles Ian Allan Publishing 2003
British Rail Fleet Survey 10: Third Rail dc Electric Multiple Units Ian Allan Publishing 1989
British Railways Pocket Book No.4 Electric Multiple Units 2013, 2017 and 2020 Platform 5 Publishing 2013/2017/2020
Cross, Derek, *Double–Headed Trains 1* Ian Allan 1979
Gough, Terry, *The Tamar and Tavy Valleys Past and Present Companion* The Nostalgia Collection 2001
Le Train Nostalgie Issue 24 Winter 2022
Marsden, C.J. and Vaughan J., *The Power of the Class 56s,* Oxford Publishing Co. 1982
Modern Locomotives Illustrated April–May 2010 Key Publishing
Modern Locomotives Illustrated April–May 2016 Key Publishing
Modern Locomotives Illustrated August–September 2009 Key Publishing
Modern Locomotives Illustrated August–September 2011 Key Publishing
Modern Locomotives Illustrated August–September 2015 Key Publishing
Modern Locomotives Illustrated December 2011–January 2012 Key Publishing
Modern Locomotives Illustrated December 2012–January 2013 Key Publishing
Modern Locomotives Illustrated December–January 2010 Key Publishing
Modern Locomotives Illustrated June –July 2013 Key Publishing
Modern Locomotives Illustrated June–July 2018 Key Publishing
Modern Locomotives Illustrated June–July 2020 Key Publishing
Modern Locomotives Illustrated October–November 2013 Key Publishing
Modern Locomotives Illustrated October–November 2015 Key Publishing
Modern Locomotives Illustrated October–November 2018 Key Publishing
Morrison B. and Vaughan J., *The Power of the Class 33s* Oxford Publishing Co. 1982
Mundy, Ian, *The Western Route new stations programme*, GWR
Railway Magazine, various issues

Scott-Morgan, Colin, *The Southern Way Special Issue* No. 18 '60 Years of the Kent Coast Electrification', Crecy Publishing Limited 2021
The Changing Face of Railfreight 2019 Mortons Media Group
The Railway Magazine, a selection of issues from 2002-2022
Today's Railways UK, various issues
Vaughan, J., *The Power of the Warships* Ian Allen Publishing Ltd 2005
Vaughan, John, *Diesel Retrospective Class 33* Ian Allan 2008
Whiteley, J.S. and Morrison, Gavin, *Profile of the Class 40s* Oxford Publishing Co. 1981
Wright, Andrew P.M., *The Swanage Branch Railway World Special* Ian Allan 1987